Mrs. Shell

Lucy Madox Brown Rossetti

Alpha Editions

This edition published in 2023

ISBN : 9789357959421

Design and Setting By
Alpha Editions
www.alphaedis.com
Email - info@alphaedis.com

Contents

PREFACE.

I have to thank all the previous students of Shelley as poet and man—not last nor least among whom is my husband—for their loving and truthful research on all the subjects surrounding the life of Mrs. Shelley. Every aspect has been presented, and of known material it only remained to compare, sift, and use with judgment. Concerning facts subsequent to Shelley's death, many valuable papers have been placed at my service, and I have made no new statement which there are not existing documents to vouch for.

This book was in the publishers' hands before the appearance of Mrs. Marshall's *Life of Mary Wollstonecraft Shelley*, and I have had neither to omit, add to, nor alter anything in this work, in consequence of the publication of hers. The passages from letters of Mrs. Shelley to Mr. Trelawny were kindly placed at my disposal by his son-in-law and daughter, Colonel and Mrs. Call, as early as the summer of 1888.

Among authorities used are Prof. Dowden's *Life of Shelley*, Mr. W. M. Rossetti's *Memoir* and other writings, Mr. Jeaffreson's *Real Shelley*, Mr. Kegan Paul's *Life of William Godwin*, Godwin's *Memoir of Mary Wollstonecraft*, Mrs. Pennell's *Mary Wollstonecraft Godwin*, &c. &c.

Among those to whom my special thanks are due for original information and the use of documents, &c., are, foremost, Mr. H. Buxton Forman, Mr. Cordy Jeaffreson, Mrs. Call, Mr. Alexander Ireland, Mr. Charles C. Pilfold, Mr. J. H. Ingram, Mrs. Cox, and Mr. Silsbee, and, for friendly counsel, Prof. Dowden; and I must particularly thank Lady Shelley for conveying to me her husband's courteous message and permission to use passages of letters by Mrs. Shelley, interspersed in this biography.

LUCY MADOX ROSSETTI.

CHAPTER I.

PARENTAGE.

The daughter of Mary Wollstonecraft and Godwin, the wife of Shelley: here, surely, is eminence by position, for those who care for the progress of humanity and the intellectual development of the race. Whether this combination conferred eminence on the daughter and wife as an individual is what we have to enquire. Born as she was at a time of great social and political disturbance, the child, by inheritance, of the great French Revolution, and suffering, as soon as born, a loss certainly in her case the greatest of all, that of her noble-minded mother, we can imagine the kind of education this young being passed through—with the abstracted and anxious philosopher-father, with the respectable but shallow-minded step-mother provided by Godwin to guard the young children he so suddenly found himself called upon to care for, Mary and two half-sisters about her own age. How the volumes of philosophic writings, too subtle for her childish experience, would be pored over; how the writings of the mother whose loving care she never knew, whose sad experiences and advice she never heard, would be read and re-read. We can imagine how these writings, and the discourses she doubtless frequently heard, as a child, between her father and his friends, must have impressed Mary more forcibly than the respectable precepts laid down in a weak way for her guidance; how all this prepared her to admire what was noble and advanced in idea, without giving her the ballast needful for acting in the fittest way when a time of temptation came, when Shelley appeared. He appeared as the devoted admirer of her father and his philosophy, and as such was admitted into the family intimacy of three inexperienced girls.

Picture these four young imaginative beings together; Shelley, half-crazed between youthful imagination and vague ideas of regenerating mankind, and ready at any incentive to feel himself freed from his part in the marriage ceremony. What prudent parents would have countenanced such a visitor? And need there be much surprise at the subsequent occurrences, and much discussion as to the right or wrong in the case? How the actors in this drama played their subsequent part on the stage of life; whether they did work which fitted them to be considered worthy human beings remains to be examined.

* * * * *

As no story or life begins with itself, so, more especially with this of our heroine, we must recall the past, and at least know something of her parents.

Mary Wollstonecraft, one of the most remarkable and misunderstood women of even her remarkable day, was born in April 1759, in or near London, of parents of whose ancestors little is known. Her father, son of a Spitalfields manufacturer, possessed an adequate fortune for his position; her mother was of Irish family. They had six children, of whom Mary was the second. Family misery, in her case as in many, seems to have been the fountainhead of her genius. Her father, a hot-tempered, dissipated man, unable to settle anywhere or to anything, naturally proved a domestic tyrant. Her mother seems little to have understood her daughter's disposition, and to have been extremely harsh, harassed no doubt by the behaviour of her husband, who frequently used personal violence on her as well as on his children; this, doubtless, under the influence of drink.

Such being the childhood of Mary Wollstonecraft, it can be understood how she early learnt to feel fierce indignation at the injustice to, and the wrongs of women, for whom there was little protection against such domestic tyranny. Picture her sheltering her little sisters and brother from the brutal wrath of a man whom no law restricted, and can her repugnance to the laws made by men on these subjects be wondered at? Only too rarely do the victims of such treatment rise to be eloquent of their wrongs.

The frequent removals of her family left little chance of forming friendships for the sad little Mary; but she can scarcely have been exactly lonely with her small sisters and brothers, possibly a little more positive loneliness or quiet would have been desirable. As she grew older her father's passions increased, and often did she boldly interpose to shield her mother from his drunken wrath, or waited outside her room for the morning to break. So her childhood passed into girlhood, her senses numbed by misery, till she had the good fortune to make the acquaintance of a Mr. and Mrs. Clare, a clergyman and his wife, who were kind to the friendless girl and soon found her to have undeveloped good qualities. She spent much time with them, and it was they who introduced her to Fanny Blood, whose friendship henceforth proved one of the chief influences of her life; this it was that first roused her intellectual faculty, and, with the gratitude of a fine nature, she never after forgot where she first tasted the delight of the fountain which transmutes even misery into the source of work and poetry.

Here, again, Mary found the story of a home that might have been ruined by a dissipated father, had it not been for the cheerful devotion of this daughter Fanny, who kept the family chiefly by her work, painting, and brought up her young brothers and sisters with care. A bright and happy example at this moment to stimulate Mary, and raise her from the absorbing and hopeless contemplation of her own troubles; she then, at sixteen, resolved to work so as to educate herself to undertake all that might and would fall on her as the stay of her family. Fresh wanderings of the restless father ensued, and finally she decided to accept a situation as lady's companion; this her hard previous life made a position of comparative ease to her, and, although all the former companions had left the lady in despair, she remained two years with her till her mother's illness required her presence at home. Mrs. Wollstonecraft's hard life had broken her constitution, and in death she procured her first longed-for rest from sorrow and toil, counselling her daughters to patience. Deprived of the mother, the daughters could no longer remain with their father; and Mary, at eighteen, had again to seek her fortune in a hard world— Fanny Blood being, as ever, her best friend. One of her sisters became housekeeper to her brother; and Eliza married, but by no means improved her position by this, for her marriage proved another unhappy one, and only added to Mary's sad observation of the marriage state. A little later she had to help this sister to escape from a life which had driven her to madness. When her sister's peace of mind was restored, they were enabled to open a school together at Stoke Newington Green, for a time with success; but failure and despondency followed, and Mary, whose health was broken, accepted a pressing invitation from her friend Fanny, who had married a Mr. Skeys, to go and stay with her at Lisbon, and nurse her through her approaching confinement. This sad visit—for during her stay there she lost her dearly loved friend—broke the monotony of her life, and perhaps the change, with sea voyage which was beneficial to her health, helped her anew to fight the battle of life on her return. But fresh troubles assailed her. Some friend suggested to her to try literature, and a pamphlet, *Thoughts on the Education of Daughters*, was her first attempt. For this she received ten guineas, with which she was able to help her friends the Bloods.

She shortly afterwards accepted a situation as governess in Lord Kingsborough's family, where she was much loved by her pupils; but their mother, who did little to gain their affection herself, becoming jealous of the ascendency of Mary over them, found some pretext for dismissing her. Mary's contact, while in this house, with people of fashion inspired her only with contempt for their small pleasures and utterly unintellectual discourse. These surroundings, although she was treated much on a footing of equality by the family, were a severe privation for Mary, who was anxious to develop her mind, and to whom spiritual needs were ever above physical.

On leaving the Kingsboroughs, Mary found work of a kind more congenial to her disposition, as Mr. Johnson, the bookseller in St. Paul's Churchyard who had taken her pamphlet, now gave her regular work as his "reader," and also in translating. Now began the happiest part of Mary's life. In the midst of books she soon formed a circle of admiring friends. She lived in the simplest way, in a room almost bare of furniture, in Blackfriars. Here she was able to see after her sisters and to have with her her young brother, who had been much neglected; and in the intervals of her necessary work she began writing on the subjects which lay nearest to her heart; for here, among other work, she commenced her celebrated *Vindication of the Rights of Woman*, a work for which women ought always to be grateful to her, for with this began in England the movement which, progressing amidst much obloquy and denunciation, has led to so many of the reforms in social life which have come, and may be expected to lead to many which we still hope for. When we think of the nonsense which has been talked both in and out of Parliament, even within the last decade, about the advanced women who have worked to improve the position of their less fortunate sisters, we can well understand in what light Mary Wollstonecraft was regarded by many whom fortunately she was not bound to consider. Her reading, which had been deep and constant, together with her knowledge of life from different points of view, enabled her to form just opinions on many of the great reforms needed, and these she unhesitatingly set down. How much has since been done which she advocated for the education of women, and how much they have already benefited both by her example and precept, is perhaps not yet generally enough known. Her religious tone is always striking; it was one of the moving factors of her life, as with all seriously thinking beings, though its form became much modified with the advance in her intellectual development.

Her scheme in the *Vindication of the Rights of Woman* may be summed up thus:—

She wished women to have education equal to that of men, and this has now to a great extent been accorded.

That trades, professions, and other pursuits should be open to women. This wish is now in progress of fulfilment.

That married women should own their own property as in other European countries. Recent laws have granted this right.

That they should have more facilities for divorce from husbands guilty of immoral conduct. This has been partially granted, though much still remains to be effected.

That, in the case of separation, the custody of children should belong equally to both parents.

That a man should be legally responsible for his illegitimate children. That he should be bound to maintain the woman he has wronged.

Mary Wollstonecraft also thought that women should have representatives in Parliament to uphold their interests; but her chief desires are in the matter of education. Unlike Rousseau, she would have all children educated together till nine years of age; like Rousseau, she would have them meet for play in a common play-ground. At nine years their capacities might be sufficiently developed to judge which branch of education would be then desirable for each; girls and boys being still educated together, and capacity being the only line of demarcation.

Thus it will be seen that Mary's primary wish was to make women responsible and sensible companions for men; to raise them from the beings they were made by the frivolous fashionable education of the time; to make them fit mothers to educate or superintend the education of their children, for education does not end or begin with what may he taught in schools. To make a woman a reasoning being, by means of Euclid if necessary, need not preclude her from being a charming woman also, as proved by the descriptions we have of Mary Wollstonecraft herself. Doubtless some of the most crying evils of civilisation can only be cured by raising the intellectual and moral status of woman, and thus raising that of man also, so that he, regarding her as a companion whose mind reflects the beauties of nature, and who can appreciate the great reflex of nature as transmitted through the human mind in the glorious art of the world, may really be raised to the ideal state where the sacrilege of love will be unknown. We know that this great desire must have passed through Mary Wollstonecraft's mind and prompted her to her eloquent appeal for the "vindication of the rights of woman."

With Mary's improved prospects, for she fortunately lived in a time when the strong emotions and realities of life brought many influential people admiringly around her, she was able to pay a visit to Paris in 1792. No one can doubt her interest in the terrible drama there being enacted, and her courage was equal to the occasion; but even this journey is brought up in disparagement of her, and this partly owing to Godwin's naïve remark in his diary, that "there is no reason to doubt that if Fuseli had been disengaged at the period of their acquaintance he would have been the man of her choice." As the little *if* is a very powerful word, of course this amounts to nothing, and it is scarcely the province of a biographer to say what might have taken place under other circumstances, and to criticise a character from that standpoint. If Mary was attracted by Fuseli's genius, and this would not have been surprising, and if she went to Paris for change of scene and thought, she certainly only set a sensible example. As it was, she had ample matter of interest in the stirring scenes around her—she with a heart to feel the woes of all: the miseries however real and terrible of the prince did not blind her to those of the peasant; the cold and calculating torture of centuries was not to be passed over because a maddened people, having gained for a time the right of power by might, brought to judgment the representatives, even then vacillating and treacherous, of ages of oppression. Her heart bled for all, but most for the longest suffering; and she was struck senseless to the ground by the news of the execution of the "twenty-one," the brave Girondins. Would that another woman, even greater than herself, had been untrammelled by her sex, and could have wielded at first hand the power she had to exercise through others; and might not France have been thus again saved by a Joan of Arc—not only France, but the Revolution in all its purity of idea, not in its horror.

In France, too, the women's question had been mooted; Condorcet having written that one of the greatest steps of progress of the human intellect would be the freedom from prejudice that would give equality of right to both sexes: and the *Requête des Dames à l'Assemblée Nationale* 1791, was made simultaneously with the appearance of Mary Wollstonecraft's *Vindication of the Rights of Woman*. These were strong reasons to attract Mary to France, strange as the time was for such a journey; but even then her book was translated and read both in France and Germany. So here was Mary settled for a time, the English scarcely having realised the turmoil that existed. She arrived just before the execution of Louis XVI., and with a few friends was able to study the spirit of the time, and begin a work on the subject, which, unfortunately, never reached more than its first volume. Her account, in a letter to Mr. Johnson, shows how acutely she felt in her solitude on the day of the King's execution; how, for the first time in her life, at night she dared not extinguish her candle. In fact, the faculty of feeling for others so acutely as to gain courage to uphold reform, does not necessarily evince a lack of sensitiveness on the part of the individual, as seems often to be supposed, but the very reverse. We can well imagine how Mary felt the need of sympathy and support, separated as she was from her friends and from her country, which was now at war with France. Alone at Neuilly, where she had to seek shelter both for economy and safety, with no means of returning to England, and unable to go to Switzerland through her inability to procure a passport, her money dwindling, still she managed to continue her literary work; and as well as some letters on the subject of the Revolution, she wrote at Neuilly all that was ever finished of her *Historical and Moral View of the French Revolution*. Her only servant at this time was an old gardener, who used to attend her on her rambles through the woods, and more than once as far as Paris. On one of these occasions she was so sickened with horror at the evidence of recent executions which she saw in the streets that she began boldly denouncing the perpetrators of such savagery, and had to be hurried away for her life by some sympathetic onlookers. It was during this time of terror around and depression within that Mary met Captain Gilbert Imlay, an American, at the house of a mutual friend.

Now began the complication of reasons and deeds which caused bitter grief in not only one generation. Mary was prompted by loneliness, love, and danger on all hands. There was risk in proclaiming herself an English subject by marriage, if indeed there was at the time the possibility of such a marriage as would have been valid in England, though, as the wife of an American citizen, she was safe. Thus, at a time when all laws were defied, she took the fatal step of trusting in Imlay's honour and constancy; and, confident of her own pure motives, entered into a union which her letters to him, full of love, tenderness, and fidelity, proved that she regarded as a sacred marriage; all the circumstances, and, not least, the pathetic way she writes to him of their child later on, prove how she only wished to remain faithful to him. It was now that the sad experiences of her early life told upon her and warped her better judgment; she who had seen so much of the misery of married life when love was dead, regarded that side, not considering the sacred relationship, the right side of marriage, which she came to understand later—too late, alas!

So passed this *année terrible*, and with it Mary's short-lived happiness with Imlay, for before the end we find her writing, evidently saddened by his repeated absences. She followed him to Havre, where, in April, their child Fanny was born, and for a while happiness was restored, and Mary lived in comfort with him, her time fully occupied between work and love for Imlay and their child; but this period was short, for in August he was called to Paris on business. She followed him, but another journey of his to England only finished the separation. Work of some sort having been ever her one resource, she started for Norway with Fanny and a maid, furnished with a letter of Imlay's, in which he requested "all men to know that he appoints Mary Imlay, his wife, to transact all his business for him." Her letters published shortly after her return from Denmark, Norway, and Sweden, divested of the personal details, were considered to show a marked advance in literary style, and from the slow modes of travelling, and the many letters of introduction to people in all the towns and villages she visited, she was enabled to send home characteristic details of all classes of people. The personal portions of the letters are to be found among her posthumous works, and these, with letters written after her return, and when she was undoubtedly convinced of Imlay's baseness and infidelity, are terrible and pathetic records of her misery—misery which drove her to an attempt at suicide. This was fortunately frustrated, so that she was spared to meet with a short time of happiness later, and to prove to herself and Godwin, both previous sceptics in the matter, that lawful marriage can be happy. Mary, rescued from despair, returned to work, the restorer, and refused all assistance from Imlay, not degrading herself by receiving a monetary compensation where faithfulness was wanting. She also provided for her child Fanny, as Imlay disregarded entirely his promises of a settlement on her.

As her literary work brought her again in contact with the society she was accustomed to, so her health and spirits revived, and she was able again to hold her place as one of its celebrities. And now it was that her friendship was renewed with that other celebrity, whose philosophy ranged beyond his age and century, and probably beyond some centuries to come. His advanced ideas are, nevertheless, what most thinking people would hope that the race might attain to when mankind shall have reached a higher status, and selfishness shall be less allowed in creeds, or rather in practice; for how small the resemblance between the founder of a creed and its followers is but too apparent.

So now Mary Wollstonecraft and William Godwin, the author of *Political Justice*, have again met, and this time not under circumstances as adverse as in November 1790, when he dined in her company at Mr. Johnson's, and was disappointed because he wished to hear the conversation of Thomas Paine, who was a taciturn man, and he considered that Mary engrossed too much of the talk. Now it was otherwise; her literary style had gained greatly in the opinion of Godwin, as of others, and, as all their subjects of interest were similar, their friendship increased, and melted gently into mutual love, as exquisitely described by Godwin himself in a book now little known; and this love, which ended in marriage, had no after-break.

But we must now again retrace our steps, for in the father of Mary Shelley we have another of the representative people of his time, whose early life and antecedents must not be passed over.

William Godwin, the seventh of thirteen children, was born at Wisbeach, Cambridgeshire, on March 3, 1756. His parents, both of respectable well-to-do families, were well known in their native place, his great-great-grandfather having been Mayor of Newbury in 1706. The father, John Godwin, became a dissenting minister, and William was brought up in all the strictness of a sectarian country home of that period. His mother was equally strict in her views; and a cousin, who became one of the family—a Miss Godwin, afterwards Mrs. Sotheran, with whom William was an especial favourite—brought in aid her strongly Calvinistic tendencies. His first studies began with an "Account of the Pious Deaths of many Godly Children"; and often did he feel willing to die if he could, with equal success, engage the admiration of his friends and the world. His mother devoutly believed that all who differed from the basis of her own religious views would endure the eternal torments of hell; and his father seriously reproved his levity when, one Sunday, he happened to take the cat in his arms while walking in the garden. All this naturally impressed the child at the time, and his chief amusement or pleasure was preaching sermons in the kitchen every Sunday afternoon, unmindful whether the audience was duly attentive or not. From a dame's school, where, by the age of eight, he had read through the whole of the Old and New Testament, he passed to one held by a certain Mr. Akers, celebrated as a penman and also moderately efficient in Latin and Mathematics. Godwin next became the pupil of Mr. Samuel Newton, whose Sandemanian views, surpassing those of Calvin in their wholesale holocaust of souls, for a time impressed him, till later thought caused him to detest both these views and the master who promulgated them. Indeed, it is not to be wondered at that so thinking a person as Godwin, remembering the rules laid down by those he loved and respected in his childhood, should have wandered far into the abstract labyrinths of right and wrong, and, wishing to simplify what was right, should have travelled in his imagination into the dim future, and have laid down a code beyond the scope of present mortals. Well for him, perhaps, and for his code, if this is yet so far beyond that it is not taken up and distorted out of all resemblance to his original intention before the time for its possible practical application comes. For Godwin himself it was also well that, with these uncongenial early surroundings, he, when the time came to think, was of the calm—most calm and unimpassioned philosophic temperament, instead of the high poetic nature; not that the two may not sometimes overlap and mingle; but with Godwin the downfall of old ideas led to reasoning out new theories in clear prose; and even this he would not give to be rashly and indiscriminately read at large, but published in three-guinea volumes, knowing well that those who could expend that sum on books are not usually inclined to overthrow the existing order of things. In fact, he felt it was the rich who wanted preaching to more than the poor.

Apart from sectarian doctrines, his tutor, Mr. Newton, seems to have given Godwin the advantage of the free range of his library; and doubtless this was excellent education for him at that time. After he had acted as usher for over a year, from the age of fifteen, his mother, at his father's death in 1772, wished him to enter Homerton Academy; but the authorities would not admit him on suspicion of Sandemanianism. He, however, gained admittance to Hoxton College. Here he planned tragedies on Iphigenia and the death of Cæsar, and also began to study Sandeman's work from a library, to find out what he was accused of. This probably caused, later, his horror of these ideas, and also started his neverending search after truth.

In 1777 he became, in his turn, a dissenting minister; until, with reading and fresh acquaintances ever widening his views, gradually his profession became distasteful to him, and in 1788, on quitting Beaconsfield, he proposed opening a school. His *Life of Lord Chatham*, however, gained notice, and he was led to other political writing, and so became launched on a literary career. With his simple tastes he managed not only for years to keep himself till he became celebrated, but he was also a great help to different members of his family; several of these did not come as well as William out of the ordeal of their strict education, but caused so little gratification to their mother and elder brother—a farmer who resided near the mother—that she destroyed all their correspondence, nearly all William's also, as it might relate to them. Letters from the cousin, Mrs. Sotheran, show, however, that William Godwin's novel-writing was likewise a sore point in his family.

In the midst of his literary work and philosophic thought, it was natural that Godwin should get associated with other men of advanced opinions. Joseph Fawcet, whose literary and intellectual eminence was much admired in his day, was one of the first to influence Godwin—his declamation against domestic affections must have coincided well with Godwin's unimpassioned justice; Thomas Holcroft, with his curious ideas of death and disease, whose ardent republicanism led to his being tried for his life as a traitor; George Dyson, whose abilities and zeal in the cause of literature and truth promised much that was unfortunately never realised: these, and later Samuel Taylor Coleridge, were acknowledged by Godwin to have greatly influenced his ideas. Godwin acted according to his own theories of right in adopting and educating Thomas Cooper, a second cousin, whose father died, ruined, in India. The rules laid down in his diary show that Godwin strove to educate him successfully, and he certainly gained the youth's confidence, and launched him successfully in his own chosen profession as an actor. Godwin seems always to have adhered to his principles, and after the success of his *Life of Chatham*, when he became a contributor to the *Political Herald*, he attracted the attention of the Whig Party, to whose cause he was so useful that Fox proposed, through Sheridan, to set a fund aside to pay him as Editor. This, however, was not accepted by Godwin, who would not lose his independence by becoming attached to any party.

He was naturally, to a great extent, a follower of Rousseau, and a sympathiser with the ideas of the French Revolution, and was one of the so-called "French Revolutionists," at whose meetings Horne Tooke, Holcroft, Stanhope, and others figured. Nor did he neglect to defend, in the *Morning Chronicle*, some of these when on their trial for high treason; though, from his known principles, he was himself in danger; and without doubt his clear exposition of the true case greatly modified public opinion and helped to prevent an adverse verdict. Among Godwin's multifarious writings are his novels, some of which had great success, especially *Caleb Williams*; also his sketch of English History, contributed to the *Annual Register*. His historical writing shows much research and study of old documents. On comparing it with the contemporary work of his friends, such as Coleridge, it becomes evident that his knowledge and learning were utilized by them. But these works were anonymous; by his *Political Justice* he became famous. This work is a philosophical treatise based on the assumption, that man, as a reasoning being, can be guided wholly by reason, and that, were he educated from this point of view, laws would be unnecessary. It must be observed here that Godwin could not then take into consideration the laws of heredity, now better understood; how the criminal has not only the weight of bad education and surroundings against him, but also how the very formation of the head is in certain cases an almost insuperable evil. He considered many of the laws relating to property, marriage, &c., unnecessary, as people guided by reason would not, for instance, wish for wealth at the expense of starving brethren. Far in the distance as the realisation of this doctrine may seem, it should still be remembered that, as with each physical discovery, the man of genius must foresee. As Columbus imagined land where he found America; as a planet is fixed by the astronomer before the telescope has revealed it to his mortal eye; so in the world of psychology and morals it is necessary to point out the aim to be attained before human nature has reached those divine qualifications which are only shadowed forth here and there by more than usually elevated natures. In fact Godwin, who sympathised entirely with the theories of the French Revolution, and even surpassed French ideas on most subjects, disapproved of the immediate carrying out of these ideas and views; he wished for preaching and reasoning till people should gradually become convinced of the truth, and the rich should be as ready to give as the poor to receive. Even in the matter of marriage, though strongly opposed to it personally (on philosophical grounds, not from the ordinary trite reasoning against it), he yielded his opinion to the claim of individual justice towards the woman whom he came to love with an undying affection, and for whom, fortunately for his theories, he needed not to set aside the impulse of affection for that of justice; and these remarks bring us again to the happy time in the lives of Godwin and Mary Wollstonecraft, when friendship melted into love, and they were married shortly afterwards, in March 1797, at old St. Pancras Church, London.

This new change in her life interfered no more with the energy for work with Mary Wollstonecraft than with Godwin. They adopted the singular, though in their case probably advantageous, decision to continue each to have a separate place of abode, in order that each might work uninterruptedly, though, as pointed out by an earnest student of their character, they probably wasted more time in their constant interchange of notes on all subjects than they would have lost by a few conversations. On the other hand, as their thoughts were worth recording, we have the benefit of their plan. The short notes which passed between Mary and Godwin, as many as three and four in a day, as well as letters of considerable length written during a tour which Godwin made in the midland counties with his friend Basil Montague, show how deep and simple their affection was, that there was no need of hiding the passing cloud, that they both equally disliked and wished to simplify domestic details. There was, for instance, some sort of slight dispute as to who should manage a plumber, on which occasion Mary seems to have been somewhat hurt at its being put upon her, as giving an idea of her inferiority. This, with the tender jokes about Godwin's icy philosophy, and the references to a little "William" whom they were both anxiously expecting, all evince the tender devotion of husband and wife, whose relationship was of a nature to endure through ill or good fortune. Little Fanny was evidently only an added pleasure to the two, and Godwin's thought of her at a distance and his choice of the prettiest mug at Wedgewood's with "green and orange-tawny flowers," testify to the fatherly instinct of Godwin. But, alas! this loving married friendship was not to last long, for the day arrived, August 30, 1797, which had been long expected; and the hopeful state of the case is shown in three little letters written by Mary to her husband, for she wished him to be spared anxiety by absence. And there was born a little girl, not the William so quaintly spoken of; but the Mary whose future life we must try and realise. Even now her first trouble comes, for, within a few hours of the child's birth, dangerous symptoms began with the mother; ten days of dread anxiety ensued, and not all the care of intelligent watchers, nor the constant waiting for service of the husband's faithful intimate friends, nor the skill of the first doctors could save the life which was doomed: Fate must wreak its relentless will. Her work remains to help many a struggling woman, and still to give hope of more justice to follow; perchance at one important moment it misled her own child. And so the mysteries of the workings of Fate and the mysteries of death joined with those of a new life.

CHAPTER II.

GIRLHOOD OF MARY—PATERNAL TROUBLES.

And now with the beginning of this fragile little life begin the anxieties and sorrow of poor Godwin. The blank lines drawn in his diary for Sunday 10th September 1797, show more than words how unutterable was his grief. During the time of his wife's patient agony he had managed to ask if she had any wishes concerning Fanny and Mary. She was fortunately able to reply that her faith in his wisdom was entire.

On the very day of his wife's death Godwin himself wrote some letters he considered necessary, nor did he neglect to write in his own characteristic plain way to one who he considered had slighted his wife. His friends Mr. Basil Montague and Mr. Marshall arranged the funeral, and Mrs. Reveley, who had with her the children before the mother's death, continued her care till they returned to the father on the 17th. Mrs. Fenwick, who had been in constant attendance on Mary, then took care of them for a time. Indeed, Mary's fame and character brought forward many willing to care for the motherless infant, whose life was only saved from a dangerous illness by this loving zeal. Among others Mr. and Mrs. Nicholson appeared with offers of help, and as early as September 18 we find that Godwin had requested Mr. Nicholson to give an opinion as to the infant's physiognomy, with a view to her education, which he (with Trelawny later) considered could not begin too soon, or as the latter said: "Talk of education beginning at two years! Two months is too late."

Thus we see Godwin conscientiously trying to bring in an imperfect science to assist him in the difficult task of developing his infant's mind, in place of the watchful love of an intelligent mother, who would check the first symptoms of ill-temper, be firm against ill-placed determination, encourage childish imagination, and not let the idea of untruth be presented to the child till old enough to discriminate for itself. A hard task enough for any father, still harder for Godwin, beset by all kinds of difficulties, and having to work in the midst of them for his and the two children's daily sustenance. Friends, and good friends, he certainly had; but most people will recognise that strength in these matters does not rest in numbers. The wet nurse needed by little Mary, though doubtless the essential necessity of the time, would not add to the domestic comfort, especially to that of Miss Louisa Jones, a friend of Harriet Godwin, who had been installed to superintend Godwin's household. This latter arrangement, again, did not tend to Godwin's comfort, as from Miss Jones's letters it is evident that she wished to marry him. Her wish not being reciprocated, she did not long remain an inmate of his house, and the nurse, who was fortunately devoted to the baby, was then over-looked from time to time by Mrs. Reveley and other ladies.

Of anecdotes of Mary's infancy and childhood there are but few, but from the surroundings we can picture the child. Her father about this time seems to have neglected all his literary work except the one of love—writing his wife's "Memoirs" and reading her published and unpublished work. In this undertaking he was greatly assisted by Mr. Skeys. Her sisters, on the contrary, gave as little assistance as possible, and ended all communication with Godwin at this difficult period of his life, and for a long while utterly neglected their poor sister's little children, when they might have repaid to some extent the debt of gratitude they owed to her.

All these complicated and jarring circumstances must have suggested to Godwin that another marriage might he the best expedient, and he accordingly set to work in a systematic way this time to acquire his end. Passion was not the motive, and probably there was too much system, for he was unsuccessful on two occasions. The first was with Miss Harriet Lee, the authoress of several novels and of *The Canterbury Tales*. Godwin seems to have been much struck by her, and, after four interviews at Bath, wrote on his return to London a very characteristic and pressing letter of invitation to her to stay in his house if she came to London, explaining that there was a lady (Miss Jones) who superintended his home. As this letter met with no answer, he tried three additional letters, drafts of all being extant. The third one was probably too much considered, for Miss Lee returned it annotated on the margin, expressing her disapproval of its egotistical character. Godwin, however, was not to be daunted, and made a fourth attempt, full of many sensible and many quaint reasons, not all of which would be pleasing to a lady; but he succeeded in regaining Miss Lee's friendship, though he could not persuade her to be his wife. This was from April to August 1798.

About the same time there was a project of Godwin and Thomas Wedgewood keeping house together; but as they seem to have much differed when together, the plan was wisely dropped. Godwin's notes in his plan of work for the year 1798 are interesting, as showing how he was anxious to modify some of his opinions expressed in *Political Justice*, especially those bearing on the affections, which he now admits must naturally play an important part in human action, though he avers his opinion that none of his previous conclusions are affected by these admissions. Much other work was planned out during this time, and many fresh intellectual acquaintances made, Wordsworth and Southey among others. His mother's letters to Godwin show what a constant drain his family were upon his slender means, and how nobly he always strove to help them when in need. These letters are full of much common sense, and though quaintly illiterate are, perhaps, not so much amiss for the period at which they were written, when many ladies who had greater social and monetary advantages were, nevertheless, frequently astray in these matters.

Godwin's novel of *St. Leon*, published in 1799, was another attempt to give the domestic affections their due place in his scheme of life; and the description of Marguerite, drawn from Mary Wollstonecraft, and that of her wedded life with St. Leon, are beautiful passages illustrative of Godwin's own happy time of marriage.

In July 1799, the death of Mr. Reveley suggested a fresh attempt at marriage to Godwin; but now he was probably too prompt, for, knowing that Mr. Reveley and his wife had not always been on the best of terms, although his sudden death had driven her nigh frantic, Godwin, relying on certain previous expressions of affection for himself by Mrs. Reveley, proposed within a month after her husband's death, and begged her to set aside prejudices and cowardly ceremonies and be his. As in the previous case, a second and a third lengthy letter, full of subtle reasoning, were ineffectual, and did not even bring about an interview till December 3rd, when Godwin and Mrs. Reveley met, in company with Mr. Gisborne. To this gentleman Mrs. Reveley was afterwards married. We shall meet them both again later on.

All this time there is little though affectionate mention of Mary Godwin in her father's diary. Little Fanny, who had always been a favourite, used to accompany Godwin on some of his visits to friends.

Many of Godwin's letters at this time show that he was not too embarrassed to be able to assist his friends in time of need; twenty pounds sent to his friend Arnot, ten pounds shortly afterwards through Mrs. Agnes Hall to a lady in great distress, whose name is unknown, prove that he was ready to carry out his theories in practice. It is interesting to observe these frequent instances of generosity, as they account to some extent for his subsequent difficulties. In the midst of straits and disappointments Godwin managed to have his children well taken care of, and there was evidently a touching sympathy and confidence between himself and them, as shown in Godwin's letters to his friend Marshall during a rare absence from the children occasioned by a visit to friends in Ireland. His thought and sincere solicitude and messages, and evident anxiety to be with them again, are all equally touching; Fanny having the same number of kisses sent her as Mary, with that perfect justice which is so beneficial to the character of children. We can now picture the scarcely three year old Mary and little Fanny taken to await the return of the coach with their father, and sitting under the Kentish Town trees in glad expectancy.

But this time of happy infancy was not to last long; for doubtless Godwin felt it irksome to have to consider whether the house-linen was in order, and such like details, and was thus prepared, in 1801, to accept the demonstrative advances of Mrs. Clairmont, a widow who took up her residence next door to him in the Polygon, Somers Town. She had two children, a boy and a girl, the latter somewhat younger than Mary. The widow needed no introduction or admittance to his house, as from the balcony she was able to commence a campaign of flattery to which Godwin soon succumbed. The marriage took place in December 1801, at Shoreditch Church, and was not made known to Godwin's friends till after it had been solemnised. Mrs. Clairmont evidently did her best to help Godwin through the pecuniary difficulties of his career. She was not an ignorant woman, and her work at translations proves her not to have been without cleverness of a certain kind; but this probably made more obvious the natural vulgarity of her disposition. For example, when talking of bringing children up to do the work they were fitted to, she discovered that her own daughter Jane was fitted for accomplishments, while little Mary and Fanny were turned into household drudges. These distinctions would naturally engender an antipathy to her, which later on would help in estranging Mary from her father's house; but occasionally we have glimpses of the little ones making themselves happy, in childlike fashion, in the midst of difficulties and disappointments on Godwin's part. On one occasion Mary and Jane had concealed themselves under a sofa in order to hear Coleridge recite *The Ancient Mariner*. Mrs. Godwin, unmindful of the delight they would have in listening to poetry, found the little ones and was banishing them to bed; when Coleridge with kind-heartedness, or the love ever prevalent in poets of an audience, however humble, interceded for the small things who could sit under a sofa, and so they remained up and heard the poet read his poem. The treat was never afterwards forgotten, and one cannot over-estimate such pleasures in forming the character of a child. Nor were such the only intellectual delights the children shared in, for Charles Lamb was among Godwin's numerous friends at this period, and a frequent visitor at his house; and we can still hear in imagination the merry laughter of children, old and young, whom he gathered about him, and who brightened at his ever ready fun. One long-remembered joke was how one evening, at supper at Godwin's, Lamb entered the room first, seized a leg of mutton, blew out the candle, and placed the mutton in Martin Burney's hand, and, on the candle being relit, exclaimed, "Oh, Martin! Martin! I should never have thought it of you."

This and such like whimsies (as when Lamb would carry off a small cruet from the table, making Mrs. Godwin go through a long search, and would then quietly walk in the next day and replace it as if it were the most natural thing for a cruet to find its way into a pocket), would break the monotony of the children's days. It was infinitely more enlivening than the routine in some larger houses, where poor little children are frequently shut up in a back room on a third floor and left for long hours to the tender mercies of some nurse, whose small slaves or tyrants they become, according to their nature. And when we remember that the Polygon at that time was touching fields and lanes, we know that little Mary must have had one of the delights most prized by children, picking buttercups and daisies, unmolested by a gardener. But during this happy age, when the child would probably have infinitely more pleasure in washing a cup and saucer than in playing the scales, however superior the latter performance may be, Godwin had various schemes and hopes frustrated. At times his health was very precarious, with frequent fainting fits, causing grave anxiety for the future. In 1803 his son William was born, making the fifth member of his miscellaneous family. At times Mrs. Godwin's temper seems to have been very much tried or trying, and on one occasion she expressed the wish for a separation; but the idea appears to have been dropped on Godwin's writing one of his very calm and reasonable letters, saying that he had no obstacle to oppose to it, and that, if it was to take place, he hoped it would not be long in hand; he certainly went on to say that the separation would be a source of great misery to himself. Either this reason mollified Mrs. Godwin, or else the apparent ease with which she might have carried out her project, made her hesitate, as we hear no more of it. Godwin, however, had occasion to write her philosophically expostulatory letters on her temper, which we must hope, for the children's sake, produced a satisfactory effect; for surely nothing can be more injurious to the happiness of children than to witness the ungovernable temper of their elders; but with Godwin's calm disposition, quarrels must have been one-sided, and consequently less damaging.

Godwin superintended the education of his children himself, and wrote many books for this purpose, which formed part of his juvenile library later on. "Baldwin's" fables and his histories for children were published by Godwin under this cognomen, owing to his political views having prejudiced many people against his name. His chief aim appears to have been to keep a certain moral elevation before the minds of children, as in the excellent preface to the *History of Rome*, where he dwells on the fact of the stories of Mucius, Curtius, and Regulus being disputed; but considers that stories—if they be no more—handed down from the great periods of Roman history are invaluable to stimulate the character of children to noble sentiments and actions. But in Godwin's case, as in many others, it must have been a difficult task counteracting the effect of example; for we cannot imagine the influence of a woman to have been ennobling who could act as Mrs. Godwin did at an early period of her married life; who, when one of her husband's friends, whom she did not care about, called to see Godwin, explained that it was impossible, as the kettle had just fallen off the hob and scalded both his legs. When the same friend met Godwin the next day in the street, and was surprised at his speedy recovery, the philosopher replied that it was only an invention of his wife. The safe-guard in such cases is often in the quick apprehension of children themselves, who are frequently saved from the errors of their elders by their perception of the consequences. Unfortunately, Mrs. Godwin's influence must have been lessened in other matters where her feeling for propriety, if with her only from a conventional and time-serving point of view, might have averted the fatal consequences which ensued later. Could she have gained the love and respect of the children instead of making them, as afterwards expressed by Mary, hate her, her moral precepts would have worked to more effect. It may have appeared to the girls, who could not appreciate the self-devotion of Godwin in acting against theories for the sake of individual justice, that the cause of all their unhappiness (and doubtless at times they felt it acutely) was owing to their father not having adhered to his previous anti-matrimonial opinions, and they were thus prepared to disregard what seemed to them social prejudices.

In the meantime Godwin struggled on to provide for his numerous family, not necessarily losing his enthusiasm through his need of money as might be supposed, for, fortunately, there are great compensations in nature, and not unfrequently what appears to be done for money is done really for love of those whom money will relieve; and so through this necessity the very love and anguish of the soul are transfused into the work. On the other hand, we see not infrequently, after the first enthusiasm of youth wears off, how the poetic side of a man's nature deteriorates, and the world and his work lose through the very ease and comfort he has attained to, so that the real degradation of the man or lowering of his nature comes more from wealth than poverty: thus what are spoken of as degrading circumstances, are, truly, the very reverse—a fact felt strongly by Shelley and such like natures who feel their ease is to be shared. We find Godwin working at his task of Chaucer, with love, daily at the British Museum, and corresponding with the Keeper of Records in the Exchequer Office and Chapter of Westminster, and Herald College, and the Librarian of the Bodleian Library; also writing many still extant letters pertaining to the subject. The sum of three hundred pounds paid to Godwin for this work was considered very small by him, though it scarcely seems so now.

Godwin found means and time occasionally to pay a visit to the country, as in September 1803, when he visited his mother and introduced his wife to her, as also to his old friends in Norwich; and during the sojourn of Mrs. Godwin and some of the children at Southend, a deservedly favourite resort of Mrs. Godwin, and later of Mrs. Shelley (for the sweet country and lovely Essex lanes, of even so late as thirty or forty years ago, made it a resort loved by artists) Godwin superintended the letter-writing of his children. We ascertain, also, from their letters to him during absence, that they studied history and attended lectures with him; so that in all probability his daughter Mary's mind was really more cultivated and open to receive impressions in after life than if she had passed through a "finishing" education at some fashionable school. It is no mere phrase that to know some people is a liberal education; and if she was only saved from perpetrating some of the school-girl trash in the way of drawing, it was a gain to her intellect, for what can be more lowering to intelligence of perception than the utterly inartistic frivolities which are supposed to inculcate art in a country out of which the sense of it had been all but eradicated in Puritan England, though some great artists had happily reappeared! Mary at least learnt to love literature and poetry, and had, by her love of reading, a universe of wealth opened to her—surely no mean beginning. In art, had she shown any disposition to it, her father could undoubtedly have obtained some of the best advice of his day, as we see that Mulready and Linnell were intimate enough to spend a day at Hampstead with the children and Mrs. Godwin during Godwin's absence in Norfolk in 1808; in fact, Charles Clairmont, as seen in his account written to his step-father, was at this time having lessons from Linnell. Perhaps Mrs. Godwin had not discovered the same gift in Mary.

At this same date we have the last of old Mrs. Godwin's letters to her son. She speaks of the fearful price of food owing to the war, says that she is weary, and only wishes to be with Christ. Godwin spent a few days with her then, and the next year we find him at her funeral, as she died on August 13, 1809. His letter to his wife on that occasion is very touching, from its depth of feeling. He mourns the loss of a superior who exercised a mysterious protection over him, so that now, at her death, he for the first time feels alone.

Another severance from old associations had occurred this year in the death of Thomas Holcroft who, in spite of occasional differences, had always known and loved Godwin well, and whose last words when dying and pressing his hands were, "My dear, dear friend." Godwin, however, did not at all approve of Hazlitt, in bringing out Holcroft's life, using all his private memoranda and letters about his friends, and wrote expostulatory letters to Mrs. Holcroft on the subject. He considered it pandering to the worst passion of the malignity of mankind.

There do not appear to be many records of the Godwin family kept during the next two or three years. Mary was intimate with the Baxters. It was Mr. Baxter whom Mrs. Godwin tried to put off by the story of Godwin's scalded legs. We also find Mary at Ramsgate with Mrs. Godwin and her brother William, in May 1811, when she was nearly fourteen years old. As Mary and Mrs. Godwin were evidently unsuited to live together, these visits, though desirable for her health, were probably not altogether pleasant times to either, to judge by remarks in Godwin's letters to his wife. He hopes that, in spite of unfavourable appearances, Mary will still become a wise, and, what is more, a good and happy woman; this, evidently, in answer to some complaint of his wife. During these years many fresh acquaintances were made by Godwin; but as they had little or no apparent influence on Mary's after career, we may pass them over and notice at once the first communications which took place between Godwin and another personage, by far the greatest in this life drama, even great in the world's drama, for now for the first time in this story we come across the name of Shelley, with the words in Godwin's diary, "Write to Shelley." Having arrived at a name so full of import to all concerned in this Life, we must yet again retrace the past.

CHAPTER III.

SHELLEY.

Shelley, a name dear to so many now, who are either drawn to him by his lyrics, which open an undreamed-of fountain of sympathy to many a silent and otherwise solitary heart, or who else are held spell-bound by his grand and eloquent poetical utterances of what the human race may aspire to. A being of this transcendent nature seems generally to be more the outcome of his age, of a period, the expression of nature, than the direct scion of his own family. So in Shelley's case there appears little immediate intellectual relation between himself and his ancestors, who seem for nearly two centuries preceding his birth to have been almost unknown, except for the registers of their baptisms, deaths, and marriages.

Prior to 1623, a link has been hitherto missing in the family genealogy—a link which the scrupulous care of Mr. Jeaffreson has brought to light, and which his courtesy places at the service of the writer. This connects the poet's family with the Michel Grove Shelleys, a fact hitherto only surmised. The document is this:—

SHELLEY'S CASE AND COKE'S REPORT, 896.

25 Sept. 1 & 2 Philip and Mary. Between Edward Shelley of Worminghurst, in the county of Sussex, Esqre., of the one part, and Rd. Cowper and Wm. Martin of the other part.

90a. Covt. to suffer recovery to enure as to Findon Manor, etc.

90b. To the use of him the said Edward Shelley and of the heirs male of his body lawfully begotten, and for lack of such issue.

To the use of the heirs male of the body of John Shelley, Esqre., sometime of Michael Grove, deceased, father to the said Edward Shelley, etc.

It will be obvious to all readers of this important document that the last clause carries us back unmistakably from the Worminghurst Shelleys to the Michel Grove Shelleys, establishing past dispute the relationship of father and son.

The poet's great grandfather Timothy, who died twenty-two years before Shelley's birth, seems to have gone out of the beaten track in migrating to America, and practising as an apothecary, or, as Captain Medwin puts it, "quack doctor," probably leaving England at an early age; he may not have found facilities for qualifying in America, and we may at least hope that he would do less harm with the simple herbs used by the unqualified than with the bleeding treatment in vogue before the Brunonian system began. Anyway, he made money to help on the fortunes of his family. His younger son, Bysshe, who added to the family wealth by marrying in succession two heiresses, also gained a baronetcy by adhering to the Whig Party and the Duke of Norfolk. He appears to have increased in eccentricity with age and became exceedingly penurious. He was evidently not regarded as a desirable match for either of his wives, as he had to elope with both of them; and his marriage with the first, Miss Michell, the grandmother of the poet, is said to have been celebrated by the parson of the Fleet. This took place the year before these marriages were made illegal. These facts about Shelley's ancestors, though apparently trivial, are interesting as proving that his forerunners were not altogether conventional, and making the anomaly of the coming of such a poet less strange, as genius is not unfrequently allied with eccentricity.

Bysshe's son Timothy seems to have conformed more to ordinary views than his father, and he married, when nearly forty, Elizabeth Pilfold, reputed a great beauty. The first child of this marriage, born on August 4, 1792, was the poet, Percy Bysshe Shelley, born to all the ease and comfort of an English country home, but with the weird imaginings which in childhood could people the grounds and surroundings with ancient snakes and fairies of all forms, and which later on were to lead him far out of the beaten track. Shelley's little sisters were the confidants of his childhood, and their sympathy must have made up then for the lack of it in his parents. Some of their childish games at diabolical processions, making a little hell of their own by burning a fagot stack, &c., shows how early his searching mind dispersed the terrors, while it delighted in the picturesque or fantastic images, of superstition. Few persons realise to themselves how soon highly imaginative children may be influenced by the superstitions they hear around them, and assuredly Shelley's brain never recovered from some of these early influences: the mind that could so quickly reason and form inferences would naturally be of that sensitive and susceptible kind which would bear the scar of bad education. Shelley's mother does not appear so much to have had real good sense, as what is generally called common sense, and thus she was incapable of understanding a nature like that of her son; and thought more of his bringing home a well-filled game bag (a thing in every way repulsive to Shelley's tastes) than of trying to understand what he was thinking; so Shelley had to pass through childhood, his sisters being his chief companions, as he had no brother till he was thirteen. At ten years of age he went to school at Sion House Academy, and thence to Eton, before he was turned twelve. At both these schools, with little exception, he was solitary, not having much in common with the other boys, and consequently he found himself the butt for their tormenting ingenuity. He began a plan of resistance to the fagging system, and never yielded; this seems to have displeased the masters as much as the boys. At Eton he formed one of his romantic attachments for a youth of his own age. He seems now, as ever after, to have felt the yearning for perfect sympathy in some human being; as one idol fell short of his self-formed ideal, he sought for another. This was not the nature to be trained by bullying and flogging, though sympathy and reason would never find him irresponsive. His unresentful nature was shown in the way he helped the boys who tormented him with their lessons; for though he appeared to study little in the regular way, learning came to him naturally.

It must not, however, be supposed that Shelley was quite solitary, as the records of some of his old schoolfellows prove the contrary; nor was he averse to society when of a kind congenial to his tastes; but he always disliked coarse talk and jokes. Nature was ever dear to him; the walks round Eton were his chief recreation, and we can well conceive how he would feel in the lovely and peaceful churchyard of Stoke Pogis, where undoubtedly he would read Gray's Elegy. These feelings would not be sympathised with by the average of schoolboys; but, on the other hand, it is not apparent why Shelley should have changed his character, as the embryo poet would also necessarily not care for all their tastes. In short, the education at a public school of that day must have been a great cruelty to a boy of Shelley's sensitive disposition.

One great pleasure of Shelley's while at Eton was visiting Dr. Lind, who assisted him with chemistry, and whose kindness during an illness seems to have made a lasting impression on the youth; but generally those who had been in authority over him had only raised a spirit of revolt. One great gain for the world was the passionate love of justice and freedom which this aroused in him, as shown in the stanzas from *The Revolt of Islam*—

Thoughts of great deeds were mine, dear friend, when first
The clouds which wrap this world from youth did pass.

There can be no doubt that these verses are truly autobiographical; they indicate a first determination to war against tyranny. The very fact of his great facility in acquiring knowledge must have been a drawback to him at school where time on his hands was, for lack of better material, frequently spent in reading all the foolish romances he could lay hold of in the neighbouring book-shops. His own early romances showed the influence of this bad literature. Of course, then as now, fine art was a sealed book to the young student. It is difficult to fancy what Shelley might have been under different early influences, and whether perchance the gain to himself might not have been a loss to the world. Fortunately, Shelley's love of imagination found at last a field of poetry for itself, and an ideal future for the world instead of turning to ruffianism, high or low, which the neglect of the legitimate outlet for imagination so frequently induces. How little this moral truth seems to be considered in a country like ours, where art is quite overlooked in the system of government, and where the hereditary owners of hoarded wealth rest content, as a rule, with the canvases acquired by some ancestor on a grand tour at a date when Puritan England had already obliterated perception;

so that frequently a few *chefs d'oeuvre* and many daubs are hung indiscriminately together, giving equal pleasure or distaste for art. This is apposite to dwell on as showing the want of this influence on Shelley and his surroundings. From a tour in Italy made by Shelley's own father the chief acquisition is said to have been a very bad picture of Vesuvius.

It is becoming difficult to realise at present, when flogging is scarcely permitted in schools, what the sufferings of a boy like Shelley must have been; sent to school by his father with the admonition to his master not to spare the rod, and where the masters left the boy, who was undoubtedly unlike his companions, to treatment of a kind from which one case of death at least has resulted quite recently in our own time. Such proceedings which might have made a tyrant or a slave of Shelley succeeded only in making a rebel; his inquiring mind was not to be easily satisfied, and must assuredly have been a difficulty in his way with a conservative master; already, at Eton, we find him styled Mad Shelley and Shelley the Atheist.

In 1810 Shelley removed to University College, Oxford, after an enjoyable holiday with his family, during which he found time for an experiment in authorship, his father authorising a stationer to print for him. If only, instead of this, his father had checked for a time these immature productions of Shelley's pen, the youth might have been spared banishment from Oxford and his own father's house, and all the misfortune and tragedy which ensued. Shelley also found time for a first love with his cousin, Harriet Grove. This also the unfortunate printing facilities apparently quashed. There is some discussion as to whether he left Eton in disgrace, but any way the matter must have been a slight affair, as no one appears to have kept any record of it; and should one of the masters have recommended the removal of Shelley from such uncongenial surroundings, it would surely have been very sensible advice.

Oxford was, in many respects, much to Shelley's taste. The freedom of the student life there suited him, as he was able to follow the studies most to his liking.

The professional lectures chiefly in vogue, on divinity, geometry, and history, were not the most to his liking—history in particular seemed ever to him a terrible record of misery and crime—but in his own chambers he could study poetry, natural philosophy, and metaphysics. The outcome of these studies, advanced speculative thought, was not, however, to be tolerated within the University precincts, and, unfortunately for Shelley, his favourite subjects of conversation were tabooed, had it not been for one light-hearted and amusing friend, Thomas Jefferson Hogg, a gentleman whose acquaintance Shelley made shortly after his settling in Oxford in the Michaelmas term of 1810. This friendship, like all that Shelley entered on, was intended to endure "for ever," and, as usual, Shelley impulsively for a time threw so much of his own personality into his idea of the character of his friend as to prepare the way for future disappointment.

Hogg was decidedly intellectual, but with a strong conservative tendency, making him quite content with the existing state of things so long as he could take life easily and be amused. His intellect, however, was clear enough to make him perceive that it is the poet who raises life from the apathy which assails even the most worldly-minded and contented, so that he in his turn was able to love Shelley with the love which is not afraid of a laugh, without the possibility of which no friendship, it has been said, can be genuine. Many are the charming stories giving a living presence to Shelley while at Oxford, preserved by this friend; here we meet with him taking an infant from its mother's arms while crossing the bridge with Hogg, and questioning it as to its previous existence, which surely the babe had not had time to forget if it would but speak—but alas, the mother declared she had never heard it speak, nor any other child of its age; here comes also the charming incident of the torn coat, and Shelley's ecstasy on its having been fine drawn. These and such-like amusing anecdotes show the genuine and unpedantic side of Shelley's character, the delightfully natural and loveable personality which is ever allied to genius. With the fun and humour were mixed long readings and discussions on the most serious and solemn subjects. Plato was naturally a great delight to him; he had a decided antipathy to Euclid and mathematical reasoning, and was consequently unable to pursue scientific researches on a system; but his love of chemistry and his imaginative faculty led him to wish in anticipation for the forces of nature to be utilised for human labour, &c. Shelley's reading and reading powers were enormous. He was seldom without a pocket edition of one of his favourite great authors, whose works he read with as much ease as the modern languages.

This delightful time of study and ease was not to endure. Shelley's nature was impelled onwards as irresistibly as the mountain torrent, and as with it all obstacles had to yield. He could not rest satisfied with reading and discussions with Hogg on theological and moral questions, and, being debarred debate on these subjects in the university, he felt he must appeal to a larger audience, the public, and consequently he brought out, with the cognisance of Hogg, a pamphlet entitled *The Necessity of Atheism*. This work actually got into circulation for about twenty minutes, when it was discovered by one of the Fellows of the College, who immediately convinced the booksellers that an *auto-da-fé* was necessary, and all the pamphlets were at once consigned to the back kitchen fire; but the affair did not end there. Shelley's handwriting was recognised on some letters sent with copies of the work, and consequently both he and Hogg were summoned before a meeting in the Common room of the College. First Shelley, and then Hogg, declined to answer questions, and refused to disavow all knowledge of the work, whereupon the two were summarily expelled from Oxford. Shelley complained bitterly of the ungentlemanly way they were treated, and the authorities, with equal reason, of the rebellious defiance of the students; yet once more we must regret that there was no one but Hogg who realised the latent genius of Shelley, that there was no one to feel that patience and sympathy would not be thrown away upon a young man free from all the vices and frivolities of the time and place, whose crime was an inquiring mind, and rashness in putting his views into print. Surely the dangers which might assail a young man thus thrown on the world and alienated from his family by this disgrace might have received more consideration. This seems clear enough now, when Shelley's ideas have been extolled even in as well as out of the pulpit.

So now we find Shelley expelled from Oxford and arrived in London in March 1811, when only eighteen years of age, alone with Hogg to fight the battle of life, with no previous experience of misfortune to give ballast to his feelings, but with a brain surcharged with mysteriously imbibed ideas of the woes of others and of the world—a dangerous age and set of conditions for a youth to be thrown on his own resources. Admission to his father's house was only to be accorded on the condition of his giving up the society of Hogg; this condition, imposed at the moment when Shelley considered himself indebted to Hogg for life for the manner in which he stood by him in the Oxford ordeal, was refused. Shelley looked out for lodgings without result, till a wall paper representing a trellised vine apparently decided him. With twenty pounds borrowed from his printer to leave Oxford, Shelley is now settled in London, unaided by his father, a small present of money sent by his mother being returned, as he could not comply with the wishes which she expressed on the same occasion. From this time the march of events or of fate is as relentless as in a Greek drama, for already the needful woman had appeared in the person of Harriet Westbrook, a schoolfellow of his sisters at their Clapham school. During the previous January Shelley had made her acquaintance by visiting her at her father's house, with an introduction and a present from one of his sisters. There seems no reason to doubt that Shelley was then much attracted by the beautiful girl, smarting though he was at the time from his rupture with Harriet Grove; but Shakespeare has shown us that such a time is not exempt from the potency of love shafts.

This visit of Shelley was followed by his presenting Harriet Westbrook with a copy of his new romance, *St. Irvyne*, which led to some correspondence. It was now Harriet's turn to visit Shelley, sent also by his sisters with presents of their pocket money. Shelley moreover visited the school on different occasions, and even lectured the schoolmistress on her system of discipline.

There is no doubt that Harriet's elder sister, with or without the cognisance of their father, a retired hotel-keeper, helped to make meetings between the two; but Shelley, though young and a poet, was no child, and must have known what these dinners and visits and excursions might lead to; and although the correspondence and conversation may have been more directly upon theological and philosophical questions, it seems unlikely that he would have discoursed thus with a young girl unless he felt some special interest in her; besides, Shelley need not have felt any great social difference between himself and a young lady brought up and educated on a footing of equality with his own sisters. It is true that her family acted and encouraged him in a way incompatible with old-fashioned ideas of gentility, but Shelley was too prone at present to rebel against everything conventional to be particularly sensitive on this point.

In May Shelley was enabled to return to his father's house, through the mediation of his uncle, Captain Pilfold, and henceforth an allowance of two hundred a year was made to him. But there had been work done in the two months that no reconciliations or allowances afterwards could undo; for while Shelley was bent on proselytising Harriet Westbrook, not less for his sisters' sake than for his own, Harriet, in a school-girl fashion, encouraged by her sister and not discouraged by her father, was falling in love with Shelley. How were the *bourgeois* father and sister to comprehend such a character as Shelley's, when his own parents and all the College authorities failed to do so? If Shelley were not in love he must have appeared so, and Harriet's family did their best by encouraging and countenancing the intimacy to lead to a marriage, they naturally having Harriet's interests more at heart than Shelley's.

However, the fact remains that Shelley was a most extraordinary being, an embryo poet, with all a poet's possible inconsistencies, the very brilliancy of the intellectual spark in one direction apparently quelling it for a time in another. In most countries and ages a poet seems to have been accepted as a heaven-sent gift to his nation; his very crimes (and surely Shelley did not surpass King David in misdoing?) have been the *lacrymæ rerum* giving terrible vitality to his thoughts, and so reclaiming many others ere some fatal deed is done; but in England the convention of at least making a show of virtues which do not exist (perhaps a sorry legacy from Puritanism) will not allow the poet to be accepted for what he really is, nor his poetry to appeal, on its own showing, to the human heart. He must be analysed, and vilified, or whitewashed in turn.

At any rate Shelley was superior to some of the respectable vices of his class, and one alleged concession of his father was fortunately loathsome to him, viz.—that he (Sir Timothy) would provide for as many illegitimate children as Percy chose to have, but he would not tolerate a *mésalliance*. To what a revolt of ideas must such a code of morality have led in a fermenting brain like Shelley's! Were the mothers to be provided for likewise, and to be considered more by Shelley's respectable family than his lawful wife? We fear not.

A visit to Wales followed, during which Shelley's mind was in so abstracted a state that the fine scenery, viewed for the first time, had little power to move him, while Harriet Westbrook, with her sister and father, was only thirty miles off at Aberystwith; a hasty and unexplained retreat of this party to London likewise hastened the return of Shelley. Probably the father began to perceive that Shelley did not come forward as he had expected, and so he wished to remove Harriet from his vicinity. Letters from Harriet to Shelley followed, full of misery and dejection, complaining of her father's decision to send her back to school, where she was avoided by the other girls, and called "an abandoned wretch" for sympathising or corresponding with Shelley; she even contemplated suicide. It is curious how this idea seems to have constantly recurred to her, as in the case of some others who have finally committed the act.

Shelley wrote, expostulating with the father. This probably only incensed him more. He persisted. Harriet again addressed Shelley in despair, saying she would put herself under his protection and fly with him; a difficult position for any young man, and for Shelley most perplexing, with his avowed hostility to marriage, and his recent assertions that he was not in love with Harriet. But it must be put to Shelley's credit that, having intentionally or otherwise led Harriet on to love him, he now acted as a gentleman to his sister's school friend, and, influenced to some extent by Hogg's arguments in a different case in favour of marriage, he at once determined to make her his wife. He wrote to his cousin, Charles Grove, announcing his intention and impending arrival in London, saying that as his own happiness was altogether blighted, he could now only live to make that of others, and would consequently marry Harriet Westbrook.

On his arrival in London, Shelley found Harriet looking ill and much changed. He spent some time in town, during which Harriet's spirits revived; but Shelley, as he described in a letter to Hogg, felt much embarrassment and melancholy. Not contemplating an immediate marriage, he went into Sussex to pay a visit to Field Place and to his uncle at Cuckfield. While here he renewed the acquaintance of Miss Kitchener, a school mistress of advanced ideas, who had the care of Captain Pilfold's children. To this acquaintance we owe a great number of letters which throw much light on Shelley's *exalté* character at this period, and which afford most amusing reading. As usual with Shelley, he threw much of his own personality into his ideas of Miss Hitchener, who was to be his "eternal inalienable friend," and to help to form his lovely wife's character on the model of her own. All these particulars are given in letters from Shelley to his friends, Charles Grove, Hogg, and Miss

Hitchener; to the latter he is very explanatory and apologetic, but only after the event.

Shelley had scarcely been a week away from London when he received a letter from Harriet, complaining of fresh persecution and recalling him. He at once returned, as he had undertaken to do if required, and then resolved that the only thing was for him to marry at once. He accordingly went straight to his cousin Charles Grove, and with twenty-five pounds borrowed from his relative Mr. Medwin, a solicitor at Horsham, he entered on one of the most momentous days of his life—the 24th or 25th August 1811. After passing the night with his cousin, he waited at the door of the coffee-house in Mount Street, watching for a girlish figure to turn the corner from Chapel Street. There was some delay; but what was to be could not be averted, and soon Harriet, fresh as a rosebud, appeared. The coach was called, and the two cousins and the girl of sixteen drove to an inn in the city to await the Edinburgh mail. This took the two a stage farther on the fatal road, and on August 28 their Scotch marriage is recorded in Edinburgh. The marriage arrangements were of the quaintest, Shelley having to explain his position and want of funds to the landlord of some handsome rooms which he found. Fortunately the landlord undertook to supply what was needed, and they felt at ease in the expectation of Shelley's allowance of money coming; but this never came, as Shelley's father again resented his behaviour, and took that easy means of showing as much.

Shelley's wife had had the most contradictory education possible for a young girl of an ordinary and unimaginative nature—the conventional surface education of a school of that time followed by the talks with Shelley, which were doubtless far beyond her comprehension. What could be the outcome of such a marriage? Had Shelley, indeed, been a different character, all might have gone smoothly, married as he was to a beautiful girl who loved him; but at present all Shelley's ideas were unpractical. Without the moral treadmill of work to sober his opinions, whence was the ballast to come when disappointment ensued— disappointment which he constantly prepared for himself by his over-enthusiastic idea of his friends? Troubles soon followed the marriage, in the nonarrival of the money; and after five weeks in Edinburgh, where Hogg had joined the Shelleys, followed by a little over a week in York, the need became so pressing that Shelley felt obliged to take a hurried journey to his uncle's at Cuckfield, in order to try and mollify his father; in this he did not succeed. Though absent little over a week, he prepared the way by his absence, and by leaving Harriet under the care of Hogg, for a series of complications and misunderstandings which never ended till death had absolved all concerned. Harriet's sister, Eliza, was to have returned to York with Shelley; but hearing of her sister's solitary state with Hogg in the vicinity, she hurried alone to York, and from this time she assumed an ascendency over the small *ménage* which, though probably useful in trifles, had undoubtedly a bad effect in the long run. Eliza, rightly from her point of view, thought it necessary to stand between Hogg and her sister. It seems far more likely that Hogg's gentlemanly instincts would have led him to treat his friend's wife with respect than that he should have really given cause for the grave suspicions which Shelley writes of in subsequent letters to Miss Hitchener. Might not Eliza be inclined to take an exaggerated view of any attention shown by Hogg to her sister, and have persuaded Harriet to the same effect? Harriet having seen nothing of the world as yet, and Eliza's experience before her father's retirement from his tavern not having been that in which ladies and gentlemen stand on a footing of equality. It is true that Shelley writes of an interview with Hogg before leaving York, in which he describes Hogg as much confused and distressed; but perhaps allowance ought to be made for the fanciful turn of Shelley's own mind. However this may have been, they left York for Keswick, where they delighted in the glorious scenery. At this time we see in letters to Miss Hitchener how Shelley felt the necessity of intellectual sympathy, and how he seemed to consider this friend in some way necessary for the accomplishment of various speculative and social ideas. Here at Chestnut Cottage novels were commenced and much work planned, left unfinished, or lost. While at Keswick he made the acquaintance of Southey and wrote his first letter to William Godwin, whose works had already had a great influence on him, and whose personal acquaintance he now sought. The often quoted letter by which Shelley introduced himself to Godwin was followed by others, and led up to the subsequent intimacy which had such important results.

Shelley with his wife and sister-in-law paid a visit to the Duke of Norfolk at Greystoke; this led to a quasi reconciliation with Shelley's father, owing to which the allowance of two hundred a year was renewed, Harriet's father making her a similar allowance, it is presumed, owing to feeling flattered by his daughter's reception by the Duchess. Shortly afterwards some restless turn in the trio caused a further move to be contemplated, and now Shelley entered on what must have appeared one of the strangest of his fancies—a visit to Ireland to effect Catholic Emancipation and to procure the repeal of the Union Act. Hogg pretends to believe that Shelley did not even understand the meaning of the phrases, and most probably many English would not have cared to do so. In any case Shelley's enthusiasm for an oppressed people must be admired, and it is noticeable that our greatest statesman of the present day has come to agree with Shelley after eighty years of life and of conflicting endeavour.

The plan adopted by Shelley caused infinite amusement to Harriet, who entered with animation into the fun of distributing her husband's pamphlets on Irish affairs, and could not well understand his seriousness on the subject.

The pamphlets and the speeches which he delivered were not likely to conciliate the different Irish parties. The Catholics were not to be attracted by an Atheist or Antichristian, however tolerant he might be of them, and of all religions which tend to good. Lord Fingal and his adherents were not inclined to follow the Ardent Republican and teacher of Humanitarianism; nor were the extreme party likely to be satisfied with appeals, however eloquent, for the pursuit and practice of virtue before any political changes were to be expected. Shelley's exposition of the failure of the French Revolution by the fact that although it had been ushered in by people of great intellect, the moral side of intellect had been wanting, was not what Irish Nationalists then wished to consider. In fact, Shelley had not much pondered the character of the people he went to help and reform, if he thought a week of these arguments could have much effect. Shelley was much sought after by the poor Irish, during another month of his stay in Dublin, on account of his generosity. Here, also, they met Mrs. Nugent. Harriet's correspondence with her has recently been published. With the views which she expresses, those of the present writer coincide in not casting all the blame of the future separation on Shelley; Harriet naturally feels Mary most at fault, and does not perceive her own mistakes. Failing in his aim, and being disheartened by the distress on all sides which he could not relieve, and more especially owing to the strong remonstrance of Godwin, who considered that if there were any result it could only be bloodshed, the poet migrated to Nantgwilt in Wales. Here the Shelleys contemplated receiving Godwin and his family, Miss Hitchener with her American pupils; and why not Miss Hitchener's father, reported to have been an old smuggler? Here Shelley first met Thomas Love Peacock. They were unable to remain at Nantgwilt owing to various mishaps, and migrated to that terrestrial paradise in North Devon, Lynmouth. This lovely place, with its beautiful and romantic surroundings loved and exquisitely described by more than one poet, cannot fail to be dear to those who know it with and through them. Here, in a garden in front of their rose and myrtle covered cottage, within near sound of the rushing Lynn, would Shelley stand on a mound and let off his fire-balloons in the cool evening air. Here Miss Hitchener joined them. What talks and what rambles they must have had, none but those who have known a poet in such a place could imagine; but perhaps Shelley, though a poet, was not sufficient for the three ladies in a neighbourhood where the narrow winding paths may have caused one or other to appear neglected and left behind. Poor Shelley, recalled from heaven to earth by such-like vicissitudes, naturally held by his wife; and forthwith disagreements began which ended in Miss Hitchener's being called henceforth the "Brown Demon." What a fall from the ideal reformer of the world!—another of Shelley's self-made idols shattered.

The Shelleys wished Fanny Godwin to join their party at Lynmouth; but this Godwin would not permit without more knowledge of his friends, although

Shelley wrote affecting letters to the sage, trusting that he might be the stay of his declining years. Amid the romantic scenery of Lynmouth, Shelley wrote much of his *Queen Mab*; he also addressed a sonnet, and a longer poem, to Harriet, in August. These poems certainly evince no falling off in affection, although they are not like the glowing love-poems of a later period.

From Lynmouth Shelley, with his party, moved to Swansea, and thence to Tremadoc, where they agreed to take a house named Tanyrallt, and then they moved on to London to meet Godwin, who, in the meanwhile, had paid a visit to Lynmouth just after their flitting. Here Shelley had the delight of seeing the philosopher face to face, and now visits were exchanged, and walks and dinners followed, and, among other friends of Godwin, Shelley met Clara de Boinville and Mrs. Turner, who is said to have inspired his first great lyric, "Away the moor is dark beneath the moon," but whose husband strongly objected to Shelley visiting their house.

On this occasion Fanny Godwin was the most seen; Mary Godwin, who was just fifteen, only arriving towards the end of Shelley's stay in London from a visit to her friends, the Baxters, in Scotland. No mention is made of her by Shelley, though she must have dined in his company about November 5, 1812. During this visit to London Shelley became reconciled with Hogg, calling on him and begging him to come to see him and his wife. This certainly does not look as if Shelley still thought seriously of his former difference with Hogg—scarcely a year before. Shortly after, on the 8th, we find the poor "Brown Demon" leaving the Shelleys, with the promise of an annuity of one hundred pounds. She reopened a school later on at Edmonton, and was much loved by her pupils. Shelley now returned to Tremadoc, where he passed the winter in his house at Tanyrallt, helping the poor through this severe season of 1812-13. Here one of Shelley's first practical attempts for humanity was assisting to reclaim some land from the sea; but Shelley's early effort, unlike the last one of Göthe's *Faust*, did not satisfy him, and shortly afterwards another real or fancied attempt on his life, on February 26th, 1813, obliged the party to leave the neighbourhood, this time again for Ireland. He spent a short time on the Lake of Killarney, with his wife and Eliza. In April we again find him in London, in an hotel in Albemarle Street; thence he passed to Half Moon Street, where in June their first child, Ianthe, was born. The baby was a great pleasure to Shelley, who, however, objected to the wet nurse. He wrote a touching sonnet to his wife and child three months later. All this time there is no apparent change of affection suggested. Soon afterwards, while at Bracknell, near Windsor, they kept up the acquaintance of the De Boinville family, and Shelley began the study of Italian with them while Harriet relinquished hers of Latin. From Bracknell Shelley paid his last visit to Field Place to see his mother, in the absence of his father and the younger children. An interview with his father followed, and a journey to Edinburgh, and then in December a return to London; certainly an ominous restlessness, caused, no doubt, considerably by want of money, but moving about did not seem the way to save or to make it. Shelley visited Godwin several times during his stay in London. At this time Shelley had to raise ruinous post-obits on the family property, and for legal reasons he now thought it desirable to follow the Scotch marriage by one in the English church, and he and Harriet were re-married on March 22, 1814, at St. George's Church.

But even now little rifts seem to have been growing, small enough apparently, and yet, like the small cloud in the sky, indicating the coming storm. This very time of trials, through want of money, seems to have been chosen by Harriet to show a hankering after luxuries which their present income could not warrant. A carriage was purchased, and was with its accompanying expenses added to the small *ménage*; silver plate was also considered a necessity; and, perhaps the thing most distasteful to Shelley's natural tastes, the wet nurse was retained, although Harriet had always appeared to be a strong young woman capable of undertaking her maternal duty. This fact was considered by Peacock to have chiefly alienated Shelley's affection.

Apart from this, poor Harriet, with the birth of her child, seems to have given up her studies, which she had evidently pursued to please Shelley, and to have awakened to the fact that it was a difficult task to take up the whole cause of suffering humanity and aid it with their slender purse, and keep their wandering household going. It is difficult to imagine the genius that could have sufficed, and it certainly needed genius, or something very like it, to keep the Faust-like mind of Shelley in any peace.

There is a letter from Fanny Godwin to Shelley, after his first visit, speaking of his wife as a fine lady. From this accusation Shelley strongly defended her, but now he felt that this disaster might really be impending. Poor pretty Harriet could not understand or talk philosophy with Shelley, and, what was worse, her sister was ever present to prevent any spontaneous feeling of dependence on her husband from endearing her to him. Even before his second ceremony of marriage with Harriet we find him writing a letter in great dejection to Hogg. He seemed really in the poet's "premature old age," as he expressed it, though none like the poet have the power of rejuvenescence. His detestation of his sister-in-law at this time was extreme, but he appears to have been incapable of sending her away. It was a perfect torture to him to see her kiss his baby. He writes thus from Mrs. de Boinville's at Bracknell, where he had a month's rest with philosophy and sweet converse. Talking was easier than acting philosophy at this juncture, and planning the amelioration of the world pleasanter than struggling to keep one poor soul from sinking to degradation; but who shall judge the strength of another's power, or feel the burden of another's woe? We can only tell how the expression of his agony may help ourselves; but surely it is worthy of admiration to find Shelley, four days after writing this most heart-broken letter to Hogg, binding his chains still firmer by remarrying, so that, come what would, no slur should be cast on Harriet.

Harriet, who had never understood anything of housekeeping, and whose *ménage*, according to Hogg, was of the funniest, now that the novelty of Shelley's talk and ways was over, and when even the constant changes were beginning to satiate her, apparently spent a time of intolerable *ennui*. It is still remembered in the Pilfold family how Harriet appeared at their house late one night in a ball dress, without shawl or bonnet, having quarrelled with Shelley. A doctor who had to perform some operation on her child was struck with astonishment at her demeanour, and considered her utterly without feeling, and Shelley's poem, "Lines, April 1814," written, according to Claire Clairmont's testimony, when Mr. Turner objected to his visiting his wife at Bracknell, gives a touching picture of the comfortless home which he was returning to; in fact, they seem to have no sooner been together again than Harriet made a fresh departure. There is one imploring poem by Shelley, addressed to Harriet in May 1814, begging her to relent and pity, if she cannot love, and not to let him endure "The misery of a fatal cure"; but Harriet had not generosity, if it was needed, and, according to Thornton Hunt, she left Shelley and went to Bath, where she still was in July. What Harriet really aimed at by this foolish move is doubtful; it was certainly taken at the most fatal moment. To leave Shelley alone, near dear friends, when she had been repelling his advances to regain her affection, and making his home a place for him to dread to come into, was anything but wise; but wisdom was not Harriet's *forte*; she needed a husband to be wise for her. Shelley, however, had most gifts, except such wisdom at this time.

Beyond these facts, there seems little but surmises to judge by. It may always be a question how much Shelley really knew, or believed, of certain ideas of infidelity on his wife's part in connection with a Major Ryan—ideas which, even if believed, would not have justified his subsequent mode of action.

But here, for a time, we must leave poor Harriet—all her loveliness thrown away upon Shelley—all Shelley's divine gifts worthless to her. What a strange disunion to pass through life with! Only the sternest philosophy or callousness could have achieved it—and Shelley was still so young, with his philosophy all in theory.

CHAPTER IV.

MARY AND SHELLEY.

We left Godwin about to write in answer to the letter referred to from Shelley. The correspondence which followed, though very interesting in itself, is only important here as it led to the increasing intimacy of the families. These letters are full of sound advice from an elderly philosopher to an over-enthusiastic youth; and one dated March 14, 1812, begging Shelley to leave Ireland and come to London, ends with the pregnant phrase, "You cannot imagine how much all the females of my family, Mrs. Godwin and *three* daughters, are interested in your letters and your history." So here, at fourteen, we find Mary deeply interested in all concerning Shelley; poor Mary, who used to wander forth, when in London, from the Skinner Street Juvenile Library northwards to the old St. Pancras Cemetery, to sit with a book beside her mother's grave to find that sympathy so sadly lacking in her home.

About this time Godwin wrote a letter concerning Mary's education to some correspondent anxious to be informed on the subject. We cannot do better than quote from it:—

Your inquiries relate principally to the two daughters of Mary Wollstonecraft. They are neither of them brought up with an exclusive attention to the system and ideas of their mother. I lost her in 1797, and in 1801 I married a second time. One among the motives which led me to choose this was the feeling I had in myself of an incompetence for the education of daughters. The present Mrs. Godwin has great strength and activity of mind, but is not exclusively a follower of the notions of their mother; and, indeed, having formed a family establishment without having a previous provision for the support of a family, neither Mrs. Godwin nor I have leisure enough for reducing novel theories of education to practice; while we both of us honestly endeavour, as far as our opportunities will permit, to improve the mind and characters of the younger branches of our family.

Of the two persons to whom your inquiries relate, my own daughter is considerably superior in capacity to the one her mother had before. Fanny, the eldest, is of a quiet, modest, unshowy disposition, somewhat given to indolence, which is her greatest fault, but sober, observing, peculiarly clear and distinct in the faculty of memory, and disposed to exercise her own thoughts and follow her own judgment. Mary, my daughter, is the reverse of her in many particulars. She is singularly bold, somewhat imperious, and active of mind. Her desire of knowledge is great, and her perseverance in everything she undertakes almost invincible. My own daughter is, I believe, very pretty. Fanny is by no means handsome, but, in general, prepossessing.

By this letter necessity appears to have been the chief motor in the education of the children. Constantly increasing difficulties surrounded the family, who were, however, kept above the lowering influences of narrow circumstances by the intellect of Godwin and his friends. Even the speculations into which Mrs. Godwin is considered to have rashly drawn her husband in the Skinner Street Juvenile Library, perhaps, for a time, really assisted in bringing up the family and educating the sons.

Before the meeting with Shelley, Mary was known as a young girl of strong poetic and emotional nature. A story is still remembered by friends, proving this: just before her last return from the Highlands preceding her eventful meetings with Shelley, she visited, while staying with the Baxters, some of the most picturesque parts of the Highlands, in company with Mr. Miller, a bookseller of Edinburgh; and he told of her passionate enthusiasm when taken into a room arranged with looking-glasses round it to reflect the magic view without of cascade and cloud-capped mountains; how she fell on her knees, entranced at the sight, and thanked Providence for letting her witness so much beauty. This was the nature, with its antecedents and surroundings, to come shortly into communion with Shelley, at the time of his despondency at his wife's hardness and supposed desertion; Shelley then, so far from self-sufficiency, yearning after sympathy and an ideal in life, with all his former idols shattered. Godwin's house became for him the home of intellectual intercourse. Godwin, surrounded by a cultivated family, was not thought less of by Shelley, owing to the accident of his then having a book-shop to look after—Shelley, whose childhood, though passed in the comforts of an English country house, yet lacked the riches of the higher culture. Through two months of various trials Shelley remained on terms of great intimacy, visiting Godwin's house and constantly dining there. This was during his wife's voluntary withdrawal to Bath, from May—when he seems to have entreated her to be reconciled to him—till July, when she, in her turn, becoming anxious at a four days' cessation of news, wrote an imploring letter to Hookham, the Bond Street bookseller, for information about her husband.

In the meantime, what had been passing in Godwin's house? The Philosopher, whom Shelley loved and revered, was becoming inextricably involved in money matters. What was needed but this to draw still closer the sympathies of the poet, who had not been exempt from like straits? He was thus in the anomalous position of an heir to twenty thousand a year, who could wish to raise three thousand pounds on his future expectations, not for discreditable gambling debts, or worse extravagances, but to save his beloved master and his family from dire distress.

What a coil of circumstances to be entangling all concerned! Mary returning from the delights of her Scottish home to find her father, whom she always devotedly loved, on the verge of bankruptcy, with all the hopeless vista which her emotional and highly imaginative nature could conjure up; and then to find this dreaded state of distress relieved, and by her hero—the poet who, for more than two years, "all the women of her family had been profoundly interested in."

And for Shelley, the contrast from the desolate home, where sulks and ill-humour assailed him, and which, for a time, was a deserted home for him; where facts, or his fitful imagination, ran riot with his honour, to the home where all showed its roseate side for him; where all vied to please the young benefactor, who was the humble pupil of its master; where Mary, in the expanding glow of youth and intellect, could talk on equal terms with the enthusiastic poet.

Were not the eyes of Godwin and his wife blinded for the time, when still reconciliation with Harriet was possible? Surely gratitude came in to play honour false. The one who—were it only from personal feeling—might have tried to turn the course of the rushing torrent was not there. Fanny, who had formerly written of Shelley as a hero of romance, was in Wales during this period.

So, step by step, and day by day, the march of fate continued, till, by the time that Hookham apparently unbandaged Godwin's eyes, on receiving Harriet's letter on July 7, 1814, passion seemed to have subdued the power of will; and the obstacle now imposed by Godwin only gave added impetus to the torrent, which nothing further could check.

Such times as these in a life seem to exemplify the contrasting doctrines of Calvin and of Schopenhauer; of two courses, either is open. But at that time Shelley was more the being of emotion than of will—unless, indeed, will be confounded with emotion.

We have seen enough to gather that Shelley did not need to enter furtively the house of his benefactor to injure him in his nearest tie, but that circumstances drew Shelley to Mary with equal force as her to him. The meetings by her mother's grave seemed to sanctify the love which should have been another's. They vaguely tried to justify themselves with crude principles. But self-deception could not endure much longer; and when Godwin forbade Shelley his house on July 8, Shelley, ever impetuous and headstrong, whose very virtues became for the time vices, thrust all barriers aside.

What deceptions beside self-deception must have been necessary to carry out so wild a project can be imagined; for certainly neither Godwin nor, still less, his wife, was inclined to sanction so illegal and unjust an act. We see, from Hogg's description, how impassioned was a meeting between Mary and Shelley, which he chanced to witness; and later on Shelley is said to have rushed into her room with laudanum, threatening to take it if she would not have pity on him. These and such like scenes, together with the philosophical notions which Mary must have imbibed, led up to her acting at sixteen as she certainly would not have done at twenty-six; but now her knowledge of the world was small, her enthusiasm great—and evidently she believed in Harriet's faithlessness—so that love added to the impatience of youth, which could not foresee the dreadful future. Without doubt, could they both have imagined the scene by the Serpentine three years later, they would have shrunk from the action which was a strong link in the chain that conduced to it.

But now all thoughts but love and self, or each for the other, were set aside, and on July 20, 1814, we find Mary Godwin leaving her father's house before five o'clock in the morning, much as Harriet had left her home three years earlier.

An entry made by Mary in a copy of *Queen Mab* given to her by Shelley, and dated in July 1814, shows us how a few days before their departure they had not settled on so desperate a move. The words are these:—"This book is sacred to me, and as no other creature shall ever look into it, I may write in it what I please. Yet what shall I write—that I love the author beyond all powers of expression, and that I am parted from him? Dearest and only love, by that love we have promised to each other, although I may not be yours I can never be another's. But I am thine, exclusively thine."

Mary in her novel of *Lodore*, published in 1835, gave a version of the differences between Harriet and Shelley. Though Lord Lodore is more an impersonation of Mary's idea of Lord Byron than of Shelley, Cornelia Santerre, the heroine, may be partly drawn from Harriet, while Lady Santerre, her match-making mother, is taken from Eliza Westbrook. Lady Santerre, when her daughter is married, still keeps her under her influence. She is described as clever, though uneducated, with all the petty manoeuvring which frequently accompanies this condition. When differences arise between Lodore and his wife the mother, instead of counselling conciliation, advises her daughter to reject her husband's advances. Under these circumstances estrangements lead to hatred, and Cornelia declares she will never quit her mother, and desires her husband to leave her in peace with her child. This Lodore will not consent to, but takes the child with him to America. The mother-in-law speaks of desertion and cruelty, and instigates law proceedings. By these proceedings all further hope is lost. We trace much of the history of Shelley and Harriet in this romance, even to the age of Lady Lodore at her separation, which is nineteen, the same age as Harriet's. Lady Lodore henceforth is regarded as an injured and deserted wife. This might apply equally to Lady Byron; but there are traits and descriptions evidently applicable to Harriet. Lady Santerre encourages her to expect submission later from her husband, but the time for that is passed. We here trace the period when Shelley also begged his wife to be reconciled to him in May, and likewise Harriet's attempt at reconciliation with Shelley, all too late, in July, when Shelley had an interview with his wife and explanations were given, which ended in Harriet apparently consenting to a separation. The interview resulted in giving Harriet an illness very dangerous in her state of health; she was even then looking forward to the birth of a child. It is true that Shelley is said to have believed that this child was not his, though later he acknowledged this belief was not correct. The name of a certain Major Ryan figures in the domestic history of the Shelleys at this time; but certainly there seems no evidence to convict poor Harriet upon, although Godwin at a later date informed Shelley that he had evidence of Harriet having been false to him four months before he left her. This evidence is not forthcoming, and the position of his daughter Mary may have made slender evidence seem more weighty at the time to Godwin; in fact, the small amount of evidence of any kind respecting Shelley's and Harriet's disagreements and separation seems to point to the curious anomaly in Shelley's character, that while he did not hesitate to act upon his avowed early and crude opinions as to the duration of marriage—opinions which he later expressed disapproval of in his own criticism of *Queen Mab*—yet the innate feeling of a gentleman forbade him to talk of his wife's real or supposed defects even to his intimate friends. Thus when Peacock cross-questioned him about his liking for Harriet, he only replied, "Ah, but you do not know how I hated her sister."

However more or less faulty, or sinned against, or sinning, we must now leave Harriet for a while and accompany Shelley and Mary on that 28th of July when she left her father's house with Jane, henceforth called "Claire" Clairmont, to meet Shelley near Hatton Garden about five in the morning. Of the subsequent journey we have ample records, for with this tour Mary also began a life of literary work, in which she was fortunately able to confide much to the unknown friend, the public, which though not always directly grateful to those who open their hearts to it, is still eager for their works and influenced by them. And so from Mary herself we learn all that she cared to publish from her journal in the *Six Weeks' Tour*, and now we have the original journal by Mary and Shelley, as given by Professor Dowden. We must repeat for Mary the oft-told tale of Shelley; for henceforth, till death separates them, their lives are together.

On July 27, 1814, having previously arranged a plan with Mary, which must have been also known to Claire in spite of her statement that she only thought of taking an early walk, Shelley ordered the postchaise, and, as Claire says, he and Mary persuaded her to go too, as she knew French, with which language they were unfamiliar. Shelley gives the account of the subsequent journey to Dover and passage to Calais, of the first security they felt in each other in spite of all risk and danger. Mary suffered much physically, and no doubt morally, having to pause at each stage on the road to Dover in spite of the danger of being overtaken, owing to the excessive heat causing faintness. On reaching Dover they found the packet already gone at 4 o'clock, so, after bathing in the sea and dining, they engaged a sailing boat to take them to Calais, and once more felt security from their pursuers; for, undoubtedly, had they been found in England, Shelley would have been unable to carry out his plan.

They were not allowed to pass the Channel together without danger, for after some hours of calm, during which they could make no progress, a violent squall broke, and the sails of the little boat were well nigh shattered, the lightning and thunder were incessant, and the imminent danger gave Shelley cause for serious thought, as he with difficulty supported the sleeping form of Mary in his arms. Surely all this scene is well described in "The Fugitives"—

While around the lashed ocean.

Though Mary woke to hear they were still far from land, and might be forced to make for Boulogne if they could not reach Calais, still with the dawn of a fresh day the lightning paled, and at length they were landed on Calais sands, and walked across them to their hotel. The fresh sights and sounds of a new language soon restored Mary, and she was able to remark the different costumes; and the salient contrast from the other side of the Channel could not fail to charm three young people so open to impressions. But before night they were reminded that there were others whom their destiny affected, for they were informed that a "fat lady" had been inquiring for them, who said that Shelley had run away with her daughter. It was poor Mrs. Godwin who had followed them through heat and storm, and who hoped at least to induce her daughter Claire to return to the protection of Godwin's roof; but this, after mature deliberation, which Shelley advised, she refused to do. Having escaped so far from the routine and fancied dulness of home life, the impetuous Claire was not to be so easily debarred from sharing in the magic delight of seeing new countries and gaining fresh experience. So Mrs. Godwin returned alone, to make the best story she could so as to satisfy the curious about the strange doings in her family.

Meanwhile the travellers proceeded by diligence on the evening of the 30th to Boulogne, and then, as Mary was far from well, hastened on their journey to Paris, where by a week's rest, in spite of many annoyances through want of money and difficulty in procuring it, Mary regained sufficient strength to enjoy some of the interesting sights. A pedestrian tour was undertaken across France into Switzerland. In Paris the entries in the diary are chiefly Shelley's; he makes some curious remarks about the pictures in the Louvre, and mentions with pleasure meeting a Frenchman who could speak English who was some help, as Claire's French does not seem to have stood the test of a lengthy discussion on business at that time. At length a remittance of sixty pounds was received, and they forthwith settled to buy an ass to carry the necessary portmanteau and Mary when unable to walk; and so they started on their journey in 1814, across a country recently devastated by the invading armies of Europe. They were not to be deterred by the harrowing tales of their landlady, and set out for Charenton on the evening of August 8, but soon found their ass needed more assistance than they did, which necessitated selling it at a loss and purchasing a mule the next day. On this animal Mary set out dressed in black silk, accompanied by Claire in a like dress, and by Shelley who walked beside. This primitive way of travelling was not without its drawbacks, especially after the disastrous wars. Their fare was of the coarsest, and their accommodation frequently of the most squalid; but they were young and enthusiastic, and could enter with delight into the fact that Napoleon had slept in their room at one inn. And the picturesque though frequently ruined French towns, with their ramparts and old cathedrals, gave them happiness and content; on the other hand, the dirt, discomfort, and ignorance they met with were extreme. At one wretched village, Echemine, people would not rebuild their houses as they expected the Cossacks to return, and they had not heard that Napoleon was deposed; while two leagues farther, at Pavillon, all was different, showing the small amount of communication between one town and another in France at that time.

Shelley was now obliged to ride the mule, having sprained his ankle, and on reaching Troyes Mary and Claire were thoroughly fatigued with walking. There they had to reconsider ways and means; the mule, no longer sufficing, was sold and a *voiture* bought, and a man and a mule engaged for eight days to take them to Neuchatel. But their troubles did not end here, for the man turned out far more obstinate than the mule, and was determined to enjoy the sweets of tyranny: he stopped where he would, regardless of accommodation or no accommodation, and went on when he chose, careless whether his travellers were in or out of the carriage. Mary describes how they had to sit one night over a wretched kitchen fire in the village of Mort, till they were only too glad to pursue their journey at 3 A.M. In fact, in those days Mary was able, in the middle of France, to experience the same discomforts which tourists have now to go much farther to find out. Their tour was far different from a later one described by Mary, when comfortable hotels are chronicled; but, oh! how she then looked back to the happy days of this time. The trio would willingly have prolonged the present state of things; but, alas! money vanished in spite of frugal fare, and they decided, on arriving in Switzerland, and with difficulty raising about thirty-eight pounds in silver, that their only expedient was to return to England in the least expensive way possible. They first tried, however, to live cheaply in an old chateau on the lake of Arx, which they hired at a guinea a month; but the discomfort and difficulties were too great, and even the customary resources of reading and writing failed to induce them to remain in these circumstances. They at one time contemplated a journey south of the Alps, but, only twenty-eight pounds remaining to live on from September till December, they naturally felt it would be safer to return to England, and decided to travel the eight hundred miles by water as the cheapest mode of transit. They proceeded from Lucerne by the Reuss, descending several falls on the way, but had to land at Loffenberg as the falls there were impassable. The next day they took a rude kind of canoe to Mumph, when they were forced to continue their journey in a return cabriolet; but this breaking down, they had to walk some distance to the nearest place for boats, and were fortunate in meeting with some soldiers to carry their box. Having procured a boat they reached Basle by the evening, and leaving there for Mayence the next morning in a boat laden with merchandise. This ended their short Swiss tour; but they passed the time delightfully, Shelley reading Mary Wollstonecraft's letters from Norway, and then, again, perfectly entranced, as night approached, with the magic effects of sunset sky, hills surmounted with ruined castles, and the reflected colours on the changing stream. They proceeded in this manner, staying for the night at inns, and taking whatever boat could be found in the morning. Thus they reached Cologne, passing the romantic scenery of the Rhine, recalled to them later when reading *Childe Harold*. From this point they proceeded through Holland by diligence, as they found travelling by the canals and winding rivers would be too slow, and consequently more expensive. Mary does not appear to have been impressed with the picturesque flat country of Holland, and gladly reached Rotterdam; but they were unfortunately detained two days at Marsluys by contrary winds, spending their last guinea, but feeling triumphant in having travelled so far for less than thirty pounds.

The captain, being an Englishman, ventured to cross the bar of the Rhine sooner than the Dutch would have done, and consequently they returned to England in a severe squall, which must have recalled the night of their departure and banished tranquillity from their minds, if they had for a time been soothed by the changing scenes and their trust in each other.

This account, taken chiefly from Mary's *Six Weeks' Tour*, published in 1817 first, differs in some details from the diary made at the time. In the published edition the names are suppressed. Nor does Mary refer to the extraordinary letter written by Shelley from Troyes on August 13, to the unfortunate Harriet, inviting her to come and stay with them in Switzerland, writing to her as his "dearest Harriet," and signing himself "ever most affectionately yours." Fortunately the proposal was not carried out; probably neither

Harriet nor Mary desired the other's company, and Shelley was saved the ridicule, or worse, of this arrangement.

CHAPTER V.

LIFE IN ENGLAND.

On leaving the vessel at Gravesend, they engaged a boatman to take them up the Thames to Blackwall, where they had to take a coach, and the boatman with them, to drive about London in search of money to pay him. There was none at Shelley's banker, nor elsewhere, so he had to go to Harriet, who had drawn every pound out of the bank. He was detained two hours, the ladies having to remain under the care of the boatman till his return with money, when they bade the boatman a friendly farewell and proceeded to an hotel in Oxford Street.

With Shelley and Mary's return to England their troubles naturally were not at an end. Instead of money and security, debts and overdue bills assailed Shelley on all sides; so much so, that he dared not remain with Mary at this critical moment of their existence, when she, unable to return to her justly indignant father, had to stay in obscure lodgings with Claire, while Shelley, from some other retreat, ransacked London for money from attorneys and on post obits at gigantic interest. We have now letters which passed between Mary and Shelley at this time; also Mary's diary, which recounts many of their misadventures.

Day after day we have such phrases as (October 22) "Shelley goes with Peacock to the lawyers, but nothing is done," till on December 21 we find that an agreement is entered into to repay by three thousand pounds a loan of one thousand. Godwin, even if he would have helped, could not have done so, as his own affairs were now in their perennial state of distress; and before long, one of Shelley's chief anxieties was to raise two hundred pounds to save Mary's father from bankruptcy, although apparently they only communicated through a lawyer. It is curious to note how Mary complains of the selfishness of Harriet; poor Harriet who, according to Mrs. Godwin, still hoped for the return of her husband's affection to herself, and who sent for Shelley, after passing a night of danger, some time before her confinement. At one time Mary entertained an idea, rightly or wrongly conceived, that Harriet had a plan for ruining her father by dissuading Hookham from bailing him out from a menaced arrest. And so we find, in the extracts from the joint diary of Mary and Shelley, Harriet written of as selfish, as indulging in strange behaviour, and even, when she sends her creditors to Shelley, as the nasty woman who compels them to change their lodgings.

Before this entry of January 2, 1815, Harriet had given birth (November 30) to a second child, a son and heir, which fact Mary notes a week later as having been communicated to them in a letter from a *deserted* wife. What recriminations and heart-burnings, neglect felt on one side and "insulting selfishness" on the other! In April, Mary writes, "Shelley passes the morning with Harriet, who is in a surprisingly good humour;" and then we hear how Shelley went to Harriet to procure his son who is to appear in one of the courts; and yet once more Mary writes, "Shelley goes to Harriet about his son, returns at four; he has been much teased by Harriet"; and then a blank as to Harriet, for the diary is lost from May 1815 to July 1816.

In the meantime we see in the diary how Mary, far from well at times, is happy in her love of Shelley—how they enjoy intellectual pleasures together. They fortunately were satisfied with each other's company, as most of their few friends fell from them, Mrs. Boinville writing a "cold and even sarcastic letter;" the Newtons were considered to hold aloof; and Mrs. Turner, whom they saw a little, told Shelley her brother considered "you've been playing a German tragedy." Shelley replied, "Very severe, but very true." About this time Hogg renewed his acquaintance with Shelley and made that of Mary, though at first his answer to Shelley's letter was far from sympathetic. On his first visit they also were disappointed with him; but a little later (November 14) Hogg called at his friend's lodging in Nelson Square, when he made a more favourable impression on Shelley by being himself pleased with Mary. She in return found him amusing when he jested, but far astray in his opinions when discussing serious matters—in fact, on a later visit of his, she finds Hogg makes a sad bungle, quite muddled on the point when in an argument on virtue. In spite of being shocked by Hogg in matters of philosophy and ethics, she gets to like him better daily, and he helps them to pass the long November and December evenings with his lively talk. On one occasion he would describe an apparition of a lady whom he had loved, and who, he averred, visited him frequently after her death. They were all much interested, but annoyed by the interruption of Claire's childish superstitions. In fact, Hogg glides back to the old friendship of the university days, and his witticisms must have beguiled many a leisure hour, while he would also help Mary with her Latin studies now commenced. Claire frequently accompanied Shelley in his walks to the lawyers and other business engagements, as Mary's health not infrequently prevented her taking long walks, and Claire stated later that Shelley had a positive fear of being alone in London, as he was haunted by the fear of an attack from Leeson, the supposed Tanyrallt assassin.

Claire's cleverness and liveliness made her a pleasant companion at times for Shelley and Mary; but even had they been sisters—and they had been brought up together as such—Mary might have found her constant presence in confined lodgings irksome, especially as Claire tormented herself with superstitious alarms which at times, even in reading Shakespeare, quite overcame her. Her fanciful imagination also conjured up causes of offence where none were intended, and magnified slight changes of mood on Shelley's or Mary's part into intentional affronts, when she ought rather to have taken Mary's delicate health and difficult position into consideration. Mary, by all accounts, seems naturally to have had a sweet and unselfish disposition, although she had sufficient character to be self-absorbed in her work, without which no work is worth doing. It is true that her friend Trelawny later appeared to consider her somewhat selfishly indifferent to some of Shelley's caprices or whims; but this was with the pardonable weakness of a man who, although he liked character in a woman, still considered it was her first duty to indulge her husband in all his freaks. However this may be, we have constantly recurring such entries in the joint diary as:—"Nov. 9.—Jane gloomy; she is very sullen with Shelley. Well, never mind, my love, we are happy. Nov. 10.—Jane is not well, and does not speak the whole day.... Go to bed early; Shelley and Jane sit up till twelve talking; Shelley talks her into good humour." Then—"Shelley explains with Clara." Again—"Shelley and Clara explain as usual."

Mary writes—"Nov. 26.—Work, &c. &c. Clara in ill humour. She reads *The Italian*. Shelley sits up and talks her into humour." Dec. 19.—A discussion concerning female character. Clara imagines that I treat her unkindly. Mary consoles her with her all-powerful benevolence. "I rise (having already gone to bed) and speak with Clara. She was very unhappy; I leave her tranquil." Clara herself writes as early as October—"Mary says things which I construe into unkindness. I was wrong. We soon became friends; but I felt deeply the imaginary cruelties I conjured up."

It is clear that where such constant explaining is necessary there could not be much satisfaction in perpetual intimacy.

Mary is amused at the way Shelley and Claire sit up and "frighten themselves" by different reasons or forms of superstition, and on one occasion we have their two accounts of the miraculous removal of a pillow in Claire's room, Claire avowing it had moved while she did not see it; and Shelley attesting the miracle because the pillow was on a chair, much as Victor Hugo describes the peasants of Brittany declaring that "the frog *must* have talked on the stone because there was the stone it talked upon." The result might certainly have been injurious to Mary, who was awakened by the excited entrance of Claire into her room. Shelley had to interpose and get her into the next room, where he informed Claire that Mary was not in a state of health to be suddenly alarmed. They talked all night, till the dawn, showing Shelley in a very haggard aspect to Claire's excited imagination (Shelley had been quite ill the previous day, as noted by Mary). She excited herself into strong convulsions, and Mary had finally to be called up to quiet her. The same effect tried a little later fortunately fell flat; but there seemed no end to the vagaries of Claire's "unsettled mind" as Shelley calls it, for she takes to walking in her sleep and groaning horribly, Shelley watching for two hours, finally having to take her to Mary. Certainly philosophy did not seem to have a calming effect on Claire Claremont's nature, and often must Shelley and Mary have bemoaned the fatal step of letting her leave her home with them. It was more difficult to induce her to return, if indeed it was possible for her to do so, with the remaining sister, Fanny, still under Godwin's roof. Fanny's reputation was jealously looked after by her aunts Everina and Eliza, who contemplated her succeeding in a school they had embarked in in Ireland. But it is not to be wondered at that the excitable, lively Clara should have groaned and bemoaned her fate when transferred from the exhilaration of travel and the beauties of the Rhine and Switzerland to the monotony of London life in her anomalous position; and although both Mary and Shelley evidently wished to be kind to her, she felt more her own wants than their kindness. Want of occupation and any settled purpose in life caused pillows and fire-boards to walk in poor Claire's room, much as other uninteresting objects have to assume a fictitious interest in the houses and lives of many fashionably unoccupied ladies of the present day, who divide their interest between a twanging voice or a damp hand and the last poem of the last fashionable poet. Shelley is not the only imaginative and simple-minded poet who could apparently believe in such a phenomenon as a faded but supernatural flower slipped under his hand in the dark, other people in whom he has faith being present, and perchance helping in the performance. Genius is often very confiding.

Peacock was perhaps the one other friend who, during these sombre, if not altogether unhappy, days of Mary, visited them in their lodgings. Shelley, through him, hears of some of the movements of his family, and at one time Mary enters with delight into the romantic idea of carrying off two heiresses (Shelley's sisters) to the west coast of Ireland. This idea occupies them for some days through many delightful walks and talks with Hogg. Peacock also frequently accompanied Shelley to a pond touching Primrose Hill, where the poet would take a fleet of paper boats, prepared for him by Mary, to sail in the pond, or he would twist paper up to serve the purpose—it must have been a relaxation from his projects of Reform.

We must not leave this delightfully unhappy time without making reference to the series of letters exchanged between Mary and Shelley during an enforced separation. Unseen meetings had to be arranged to avoid encounters with bailiffs, at a time when the landlady refused to send them up dinner, as she wanted her money, and Shelley, after a hopeless search for money, could only return home—with cake. During this time some of their most precious letters were written to each other. We cannot refrain from quoting some touching passages after Mary had received letters from Shelley expressing the greatest impatience and grief at his separation from her, appointing vague meeting-places where she had to walk backwards and forwards from street to street, in the hopes of a meeting, and fearful animosity against the whole race of lawyers, money-lenders, &c., though all his hopes depended on them at the time. The London Coffee House seemed to be the safest meeting-place.

Mary, not very clear about business matters at the time, felt most the separation from her husband: the dangers that surrounded them she only felt in a reflected way through him. They must have confidence in each other, she thinks, and their troubles cannot but pass, for there is certainly money which must come to them!

She thus writes (October 25):

For what a minute did I see you yesterday! Is this the way, my beloved, we are to live till the 6th? In the morning when I wake, I turn to look for you. Dearest Shelley, you are solitary and uncomfortable. Why cannot I be with you, to cheer you and press you to my heart? Ah! my love, you have no friends. Why then should you be torn from the only one who has affection for you? But I shall see you to-night, and this is the hope that I shall live on through the day. Be happy, dear Shelley, and think of me! Why do I say this, dearest and only one? I know how tenderly you love me, and how you repine at your absence from me. When shall we be free from fear of treachery? I send you the letter I told you of from Harriet, and a letter we received yesterday from Fanny (this letter made an appointment for a meeting between Fanny and Clara); the history of this interview I will tell you when I come, but, perhaps as it is so rainy a day, Fanny will not be allowed to come at all. I was so dreadfully tired yesterday that I was obliged to take a coach home. Forgive this extravagance; but I am so very weak at present, and I had been so agitated through the day, that I was not able to stand; a morning's rest, however, will set me quite right again; I shall be well when I meet you this evening. Will you be at the door of the coffee-house at five o'clock, as it is disagreeable to go into such places? I shall be there exactly at that time, and we can go into St. Paul's, where we can sit down.

I send you "Diogenes," as you have no books; Hookham was so ill-tempered as not to send the book I asked for.

Two more distracted letters from Shelley follow, showing how he had been in desperation trying to get money from Harriet; how pistols and microscope were taken to a pawnshop; Davidson, Hookham, and others are the most hopeless villains, but must be propitiated. Trying letters also arrive from Mrs. Godwin, who was naturally much incensed with Mary, and of whom Mary expresses her detestation in writing to Shelley. One more short letter:

October 27.

MY OWN LOVE,

I do not know by what compulsion I am to answer you, but your letter says I must; so I do.

By a miracle I saved your £5, and I will bring it. I hope, indeed, oh, my loved Shelley, we shall indeed be happy. I meet you at three, and bring heaps of Skinner St. news.

Heaven bless my love and take care of him.

HIS OWN MARY.

As many as three and four letters in a day pass between Shelley and Mary at this time. Another tender, loving letter on October 28, and then they decide on the experiment of remaining together one night. Warned by Hookham, who regained thus his character for feeling, they dared not return to the London Tavern, but took up their abode for a night or two at a tavern in St. John Street. Soon the master of this inn also became suspicious of the young people, and refused to give more food till he received money for that already given; and again they had to satisfy their hunger with cakes, which Shelley obtained money from Peacock to purchase. Another day in the lodgings where the landlady won't serve dinner, cakes again supplying the deficiency. Still separation, Shelley seeking refuge at Peacock's. Fresh letters of despair and love, Godwin's affairs causing great anxiety and efforts on Shelley's part to extricate him. A Sussex farmer gives fresh hope. On November 3 Mary writes very dejectedly. She had been *nearly* two days without a letter from Shelley, that is, she had received one of November 2 early in the morning, and that of November 3 late in the evening. That day had also brought Mary a letter from her old friends the Baxters, or rather from Mr. David Booth, to whom her friend Isabel Baxter was engaged, desiring no further communication with her. This was a great blow to Mary, as, Isabel having been a great admirer of Mary Wollstonecraft, Mary had hoped she would remain her friend. Mary writes:—"She adores the shade of my mother. But then a married man! It is impossible to knock into some people's heads that Harriet is selfish and unfeeling, and that my father might be happy if he chose. By that cant of selling his daughter, I should half suspect that there has been some communication between the Skinner Street folks and them."

But now the separation was approaching its end, and the danger of being arrested past, they move from their lodgings in Church Terrace, St. Pancras, to Nelson Square, where we have already seen Hogg in their company and heard of the sulks, fears, and bemoanings of poor Claire.

Mary Shelley's novel of *Lodore* gives a good account of the sufferings of this time, as referred to later. The great resource of intellectual power is manifested during all this period. During a time of ill-health, anxieties of all kinds, constant moves from lodgings where landladies refused to send up dinner, while she was discarded by all her friends, while she had to walk weary distances, dodging creditors, to get a sight from time to time of her loved Shelley, while Claire bemoaned her fate and seems to have done her best to have the lion's share of Shelley's intellectual attention (for she partook in all the studies, was able to take walks, and kept him up half the night "explaining"), Mary indefatigably kept to her studies, read endless books, and made progress with Latin, Greek, and Italian. In fact, she was educating herself in a way to subsist unaided hereafter, to bring up her son, and to fit him for any position that might come to him in this world of changing fortunes. Whatever faults Mary may have had, it is not the depraved who prepare themselves for, and honestly fight out, the battle of life as she did.

CHAPTER VI.

DEATH OF SHELLEY'S GRANDFATHER, AND BIRTH OF A CHILD.

After Shelley had freed himself, for a time, of some of his worst debts towards the close of 1814, the year 1815, with the death of his grandfather on January 6, brought a prospect of easier circumstances, as he was now his father's immediate heir.

Although Shelley was not invited to the funeral, and only knew of the death through the papers, he determined at once to go into Sussex, with Claire as travelling companion, as Mary was not well enough for the journey. Shelley left Claire at Slinfold, and proceeded alone to his father's house, where he was refused admittance; so he adopted the singular plan of sitting in the garden, before the door, passing the time by reading *Comus*. One or two friends come out to see him, and tell him his father is very angry with him, and the will is most extraordinary; finally he is referred to Sir Timothy's solicitor—Whitton. From him, Mary writes in her diary, Shelley hears that if he will entail the estate he is to have the income of one hundred thousand pounds.

The property was really left in this way, as explained by Professor Dowden. Sir Bysshe's possessions did not, probably, fall short of £200,000. One portion, valued at £80,000, consisted of certain entailed estates, but without Shelley's concurrence the entail could not be prolonged beyond himself; the rest consisted of unentailed landed property and personal property amounting to £120,000. Sir Bysshe desired that the whole united property should pass from eldest son to eldest son for generations. This arrangement, however, could not be effected without Shelley. Sir Bysshe, in his will, offered his grandson not only the rentals, but the income of the great personal property, if he would renew the entail of the settled property and would also consent to entail the unsettled property; otherwise he should only receive the entailed property, which was bound to come to him, and which he could dispose of at his pleasure, should he survive his father. He had one year to make his choice in.

Shelley is considered to have been business-like in his negotiations; but to have retained his original distaste of 1811 to entailing large estates to descend to his children—in fact, he appears to have considered too little the contingency of what would come to them or to Mary in the event of his death prior to that of his father. Pressing present needs being paramount at this time, he agreed to an arrangement by which a portion of the estate valued at £18,000 could be disposed of to his father for £11,000, and an income of £1,000 a year secured to Shelley during his and his father's life. At one time there was an idea of disposing of the entailed estate to his father, as a reversion, but this was not sanctioned by the Court of Chancery. Money was also allowed by his father to pay his debts.

So now we see Mary and Shelley with one thousand pounds a year, less two hundred pounds which, as Shelley ordered, was to be paid to Harriet in quarterly instalments.

Now that the money troubles were over, which for a time absorbed their whole attention, Mary began to perceive signs of failing health in Shelley, and one doctor asserted that he had abscesses on the lungs, and was rapidly dying of consumption. Whatever these symptoms were really attributable to they rapidly disappeared, although Shelley was a frequent sufferer in various ways through his life.

In February, we see also the effect of the mental strain and fatigue on Mary, as she gave birth, about the 22nd of that month, to a seven-months' child, a little girl, who only lived a few days, but long enough to win her mother's and father's love, and leave the first blank in their lives. The diary of this time, kept up first by Claire, and then by Mary, gives some details of the baby's short life. On February 22—

Mary is well and at ease, the child not expected to live, Shelley sits up with Mary. Much agitated and exhausted. Hogg sleeps here.

23.—Mary well; child unexpectedly alive. Fanny comes and stays the night.... 24.—Mary still well; favourable symptoms of the child. Dr. Clarke confirms our hope.... Hogg comes in evening. Shelley unwell and exhausted. 25.— Child and Mary very well. Shelley is very unwell. 26.—Mary rises to-day. Hogg calls; talk. Mary retires at 6 o'clock.... Shelley has a spasm. On 27 Shelley and Clara go about a cradle. 28.—Mary goes down-stairs; nurses the baby, and reads *Corinne* and works. Shelley goes to consult Dr. Pemberton. On March 1st nurse baby, read *Corinne*, and work. Peacock and Hogg call; stay till half-past eleven.

On March 2 they move to fresh lodgings. It is uncertain whether it was to 26 Marchmont Street, from which place letters are addressed in April and May. or whether they were in some other lodgings in the interval. This early move was probably detrimental to Mary and the baby, for on March 6 we find the entry: "Find my baby dead. Send for Hogg. Talk. A miserable day."

Mary thinks, and talks, and dreams of her little baby, and finds reading the best palliative to her grief.

March 19.—Dream that my little baby came to life again; that it had only been cold, and that we rubbed it before the fire, and it lived. Awake to find no baby. I think about the little thing all day. Not in good spirits. Shelley is very unwell.

March 20.—Dream again about my little baby.

Mrs. Godwin had sent a present of linen for the infant, and Fanny Godwin repeated her visits; but the little baby, who might have been a link towards peace with the Godwins, has escaped from a world of sorrow, where, in spite of a mother's love, she might later on have met with a cold reception.

Godwin at this time was in the anomalous position of communicating with Shelley on his business matters; but for the very reason that Shelley lent him, or gave him, money, he felt it the more necessary to hold back from friendly intercourse, or from seeing his daughter—a curious result of philosophic reasoning, which appears more like worldly wisdom.

From this time the company of Claire was becoming insufferable to Mary and Shelley. At least for a time, it was desirable to have a change. We find Mary sorely puzzled in her diary at times, as on March 11 she writes—"Talk about Clara's going away; nothing settled. I fear it is hopeless. She will not go to Skinner Street; then our house is the only remaining place I plainly see. What is to be done?

March 12.—"Talk a great deal. Not well, but better. Very quiet in the morning and happy, for Clara does not get up till four...." Again on the 14th March—"The prospect appears more dismal than ever; not the least hope. This is, indeed, hard to bear."

At one time Godwin, Shelley, and Mary tried to induce Mrs. Knapp to take her, but she refused. Claire also tried to get a place as companion, but that fell through, till at length the bright idea occurred to them of sending her into Devonshire, under the excuse of her needing change of air; and there, according to a letter from Mrs. Godwin to Lady Mountcashell, she was placed with a Mrs. Bicknall, the widow of a retired Indian officer. Two more entries in Mary's journal, of this time, show with what feelings of relief she contemplates the departure of Shelley's friend, as she now calls Claire. Noting that Shelley and his friend have their last talk, the next day, May 13, Shelley walks with her, and she is gone! and Mary begins "a new diary with our regeneration."

There is a letter from Claire to Fanny Godwin, of May 28, apparently from Lynmouth, describing the scenery in a very picturesque manner, and saying how she delights in the peace and quiet of the country after the turmoil of passion and hatred she had passed through. She also expresses delight that their father had received one thousand pounds—this was evidently part of what Shelley had undertaken to pay for him, and was included in the sum which Sir Timothy paid for his debts. Claire—or Jane, as she was still called in Skinner Street—supposed her family would be comfortable for a month or two.

Shelley and Mary now yearned for the country, and truly their eight months' experience in London had been a trying period, from various causes, but redeemed by their love and intellectual conversation. Now they felt unencumbered by pressing money troubles, and free from the burden of Claire's still more trying presence, at least to Mary. In June we find them together at Torquay, and we can imagine the delight of the poet and his loved Mary in their first unshared companionship—the quiet rambles by sea and cliff in the long June evenings, the sunsets, the quiet and undisturbed peace which surrounded them. They were able to give each other quaint pet names, which no one could or need understand—which would have sounded silly in the presence of a third person. This was a time in which they could grow really to know each other without reserve, when there need be no jealous competition as to who was most proficient in Greek or Latin; when Shelley was drawn to poetry, and *Alastor* was contemplated, the melancholy strain of which seems to indicate love as the only redeeming element of life, and which might well follow the time of turmoil in Shelley's career. May not this poem have been his self-vindication as exhibiting what he might have become had he not followed the dictates of his heart? "Pecksie" and the "Elfin Knight" were the names which still stand written at the end of the first journal, ending with Claire's departure. Mary added some useful receipts for future use. One is: "A tablespoonful of the spirit of aniseed, with a small quantity of spermaceti;" to which Shelley adds the following: "9 drops of human blood, 7 grains of gunpowder, 1/2 oz. of putrified brain, 13 mashed grave-worms—the Pecksie's doom salve. The Maie and her Elfin Knight."

We next find Mary at Clifton, July 27, 1815, writing in much despondency at being alone while Shelley is house-hunting in South Devon. Although she wishes to have a home of her own, she dreads the time it will take Shelley to find it. He ought to be with her the next day, the anniversary of their journey to Dover; without him it will be insupportable. And then the 4th of August will be his birthday, when they must be together. They might go to Tintern Abbey. If Shelley does not come to her, or give her leave to join him, she will leave in the morning and be with him before night to give him her present with her own hand. And then, is not Claire in North Devon? If Shelley has let her know where he is, is she not sure to join him if she think he is alone? Insufferable thought! As Professor Dowden shows, Mary must have been very soon joined by Shelley after this touching appeal. In all probability a house was fixed on, but in a very opposite direction, before the end of the week, and the lease or arrangements made by August 3, as the following year he writes from Geneva to Langdill to give up possession of his house at Bishopsgate by August 3, 1816. So here, far from Devonshire, by the gates of Windsor Forest, near the familiar haunts of his Eton days, we again find Shelley and Mary. Here Peacock was not far distant at Marlow, and Hogg could arrive from London, and here they were within reach of the river. No long time elapsed before they were tempted to experience again the delights of a holiday on the Thames. So Mary and Shelley, with Peacock and Charles Clairmont to help him with an oar, embarked and went up the river. They passed Reading and Oxford, winding through meadows and woods, till arriving at Lechlade, fourteen miles from the source of the Thames, they still strove to help the boat to reach this point if the boat would not help them. This proved impossible. After three miles, as cows had taken possession of the stream, which only covered their hoofs, the party had perforce to return, still contemplating proceeding by canal and river, even as far as the Clyde, the poet ever yearning forwards. But this, money and prudence forbade, as twenty pounds was needed to pass the first canal; so they returned to their pleasant furnished house at Bishopsgate. On this trip Mary saw Shelley's old quarters at Oxford, where they spent a night, and they must have lingered in Lechlade Churchyard, as the sweet verses there written indicate. Shelley and Mary were now settled for the first time in a home of their own: she was making rapid progress with Latin, having finished the fifth book of the Aeneid, much to Shelley's satisfaction, as recounted in a letter to Hogg. Hogg was expected to stay with them in October, and in the meanwhile, under the green shades of Windsor Forest, Shelley was writing his *Alastor*, and, as his wife describes in her edition of his poems, "The magnificent woodland was a fitting study to inspire the various descriptions of forest scenery we find in the poem." She writes:—

None of Shelley's poems is more characteristic than this. The solemn spirit that exists throughout, the worship of the majesty of nature, and the breedings of a poet's heart in solitude—the mingling of the exulting joy which the various aspects of the visible universe inspire with the sad and trying pangs which human passion imparts—give a touching interest to the whole. The death which he had often contemplated during the last months as certain and near, he here represented in such colours as had, in his lonely musings, soothed his soul to peace. The versification sustains the solemn spirit which breathes throughout; it is peculiarly melodious. The poem ought rather to be considered didactic than narrative; it was the outpouring of his own emotions, embodied in the purest form he could conceive, painted in the ideal hues which his brilliant imagination inspired, and softened by the recent anticipation of death.

Poetry was theirs, Nature their mutual love: Nature and two or three friends, if we may include the Quaker, Dr. Pope, who called on Shelley and wished to discuss theology with him, and when Shelley said he feared his views would not be to the Doctor's taste replied "I like to hear thee talk, friend Shelley. I see thou art very deep." But beyond these all friends had fallen off, and certainly Godwin's conduct seems to have been most extraordinary. He did not hesitate to put Shelley to considerable inconvenience for money, for not long after the one thousand pounds had been given, we find Shelley having to sell an annuity to help him with more money. Yet Godwin all this time treated Shelley and Mary with great haughtiness, much to their annoyance, though neither let it interfere with the duty they owed Godwin as father and philosopher. These perpetual worries helped to keep them in an unsettled state in their home. Owing perhaps to the loss of the diary at this period, we have no information about Harriet. Already in January, we find there is an idea of residing in Italy, both for the sake of health, and on account of the annoyance they experienced from their general treatment. Shelley had the poet's yearning for sympathy, and Mary must have suffered with and for him, especially when her father, for whom he did so much, treated him with haughty severity by way of thanks. Mary attributed Godwin's conduct to the influence of his wife, whom she cordially disliked at this time. She was loth to recognise inconsistency in her father, whom she always revered. Godwin on his side was by no means anxious for his daughter and Shelley to leave for Italy in a few weeks' time, as intimated to him by Shelley as possible on the 16th February. We thus see that a trip to the Continent was contemplated some months prior to the journey to Geneva. This idea arose after the birth of Mary's first son, William, born January 24, 1816, who was destined to be only for a few short years the joy of his parents, and then to rest in Rome, where Shelley was not long in following him.

It is evident from Godwin's diary that Claire must have been on a visit or in direct communication with Mary at the beginning of January, as Godwin notes "Write to P.B.S. inviting Jane"; and it does not seem to have been possible for Shelley and Mary to have borne resentment. The facts of this meeting early in the year, and that Mary and Shelley contemplated another of their restless journeys abroad, certainly take off from the abruptness of their departure for Geneva in May with Claire Claremout. Undoubtedly Shelley was in a worried and excited state at this period, and he acted so as to rouse the doubts of Peacock as to the reason of the hurried journey. The story of Williams of Tremadock suddenly appearing at Bishopsgate, to warn Shelley that his father and uncle were engaged in a plot to lock him up, seems without foundation. But when, in addition to this story, we consider Claire's history, we can well understand that, in spite of Shelley's love of sincerity and truth, circumstances were too strong for him. At a time when he and Mary were being avoided by society for openly defying its laws, they might well reflect whether they could afford to avow the new complication which had sprung up in their small circle. Claire, in hopes of finding some theatrical engagement, had called upon Lord Byron at Drury Lane Theatre, apparently about March 1816, during the distressing period of his rupture with his wife.

The result of this acquaintance is too well known, and has been too much a source of obloquy to all concerned in it, to need much comment here, and it is only as the facts affect Mary that we need refer to them at all.

At this time Byron was about to leave England, pursued, justly or unjustly, by the hatred of the British mob for a poet who dared to quarrel with his wife and follow the low manners of some of the leaders of fashion whom he had been intimate with. Their obscurity has sheltered *them* from opprobrium. He was accompanied by the young physician, Dr. John Polidori, who has somehow passed with Byron's readers as a fool; yet he certainly could have been no fool in the ordinary sense of the word, as he had taken full degrees as a doctor at an earlier age perhaps than had ever been known before. His family, a simple and highly educated family (his father was Italian, and had been secretary to Alfieri), caring very much for poetry and intellectual intercourse, were delighted at the prospect of the young physician having such an opening to his career, as his sister, the mother of poets, has told the writer. It is true that this exciting short period with Byron must have had an injurious effect on the young physician's after career, though he was still able to obtain the deep interest of Harriet Martineau at Norwich. It might be added that his nephew, not only a poet but a leader in poetic thought, deeply resented the insulting terms in which Byron wrote of Polidori, and, although h deeply admired the genius of Byron, did not fail to note where any weakness of form could be found in his work—such is human nature, and so is poetic justice meted out. This might appear to be a slight digression from our subject, if it were not for the fact that when Mary wrote *Frankenstein* at Sécheron, as one of the tales of horror that were projected by the assembled party, it was only John Polidori's story of *The Vampire* which was completed along with Mary's *Frankenstein*, *The Vampire*, published anonymously, was at first extolled everywhere under the idea that it was Byron's, and when this idea was found to be a mistake the tale was slighted in proportion, and its author with it. The fact is that as an imaginative tale of horror *The Vampire* holds its place beside Mary's *Frankenstein*, though not so fully developed as a literary performance or as an invention.

So on the eve of Byron's starting for Switzerland, we find Shelley and Mary contemplating a journey with Claire in the same direction by another route, but to the same place and hotel, previously settled on and engaged by Byron. It certainly might appear that Shelley and Mary in this dilemma did not feel justified in acting towards another in a way contrary to their own conduct in life. In all probability Claire confided her belief in Byron's attachment to herself, after his wife had discarded him, to Mary or even to Shelley. Mary, however distasteful the subject must have been to her, would not perhaps allow herself to stand in the way of what, from her own experience, might appear to be a prospect of a settlement in life for Claire, especially as she must deeply have felt their responsibility in having induced or allowed her to accompany them in their own elopement. In fact, the feeling of responsibility in this most trying case might, to a highly imaginative mind, almost conjure up the invention of a Frankenstein.

We now (May 3, 1816) find Shelley, Mary, and Claire at Dover, again on a journey to Switzerland. From Dover Shelley wrote a kind letter to Godwin, explaining money matters, and promising to do all he could to help him. They pass by Paris, then by Troyes, Dijon, and Dôle, through the Jura range. This time is graphically described by Shelley in letters appended to the *Six Weeks' Tour,* the journey and the eight days' excursion in Switzerland. We read of the terrific changes of nature, the thunderstorms, one of which was more imposing than all the others, lighting up lake and pine forests with the most vivid brilliancy, and then nothing but blackness with rolling thunder. These letters are addressed to Peacock, but in them we have no reference to the intimacy with Byron now being carried on; how he arrived at the Hotel Sécheron, nor their removal to the Maison Chapuis to avoid the inquisitive English.

There is, fortunately, no further reason to refer to the rumours which scandal-mongers promulgated—rumours which undoubtedly hastened the rupture between Byron and Claire; although evil rumours, like fire smouldering in a hold, are difficult to extinguish, and, as Mr. Jeaffreson shows, the slanders of this time were afterwards a trouble to Shelley at Ravenna, in 1821, when his wife had to take his part. These rumours were the source of certain poems, and also, later, stories about Byron. All lovers of Shelley owe a debt of deep gratitude to Mr. Jeaffreson, who, although, severe to a fault on many of the blemishes in his character (as if he considered that poets ought to be almost superhuman in all things), nevertheless proves in so clear a way the utter groundlessness of the rumours as to relieve all future biographers from considering the subject. At the same time he shows how distasteful Claire's presence must have become to Byron, who was hoping for reconciliation with his wife, and who naturally construed fresh obduracy on her part as the result of reports that were becoming current. Anyway, it is manifest that Byron did not regard Claire in the light that Mary may have hoped for—namely, that he would consider her as a wife, taking the place of her who had left him. Byron had no such new idea of the nature of a wife, but only accepted Claire as she allowed herself to be taken, with the addition that he grew to dislike her intensely.

So after Shelley and Byron had made their eight days' tour of the lake, from June 23, unaccompanied by Mary and Claire, we find a month later Shelley taking them for an eight days' tour to Chamouni, unaccompanied by Byron. Of this tour Shelley each day writes long descriptive letters to Peacock, who is looking out for a house for them somewhere in the neighbourhood of

Windsor. They return by July 28 to Montalègre, where he writes of the collection of seeds he has been making, and which Mary intends cultivating in her garden in England.

For another month these young restless beings enjoy the calm of their cottage by the lake, close to the Villa Diodati, while the poets breathe in poetry on all sides, and give it to the world in verse. Mary notes the books they read, and their visits in the evening to Diodati, where she became accustomed to the sound of Byron's voice, with Shelley's always the answering echo, for she was too awed and timid to speak much herself. These conversations caused her, subsequently, when hearing Byron's voice, to feel a sad want for "the sound of a voice that is still."

It is during this sojourn by the Swiss Lake that Mary began her first serious attempt at literature. Being asked each day by Shelley whether she had found a story, she answered "No," till one evening after listening to a conversation between Byron and Shelley on the principle of life—whether it would be discovered, and the power of communicating life be acquired—"perhaps a corpse might be reanimated; galvanism had given tokens of such things"— she lay awake, and with the sound of the lake and the sight of the moonlight gleaming through chinks in the shutters, were blended the idea and the figure of a student engaged in the ghastly work of creating a man, until such a horror came to light that he shrank in fear from his own performance. Such was the original idea for this imaginative work of a girl of nineteen, which has held its place among conspicuous works of fiction to the present day. *Frankenstein* was the outcome of the project before mentioned of writing tales of horror. One night, when pouring rain detained Shelley's party at the Villa Diodati over a blazing fire, they told strange stories, till Byron, leading to poetic ideas, recited the witch's scene from "Christabel," which so excited Shelley's imagination that he shrieked, and ran from the room; and Polidori writes that he brought him to by throwing water in his face. Upon his reviving, they agreed to write each a supernatural tale. Matthew Gregory Lewis, the author of *The Monk*, who visited at Diodati, assisted them with these weird fancies.

CHAPTER VII.

"FRANKENSTEIN."

That a work by a girl of nineteen should have held its place in romantic literature so long is no small tribute to its merit; this work, wrought under the influence of Byron and Shelley, and conceived after drinking in their enthralling conversation, is not unworthy of its origin. A more fantastically horrible story could scarcely be conceived; in fact, the vivid imagination, piling impossible horror upon horror, seems to claim for the book a place in the company of a Poe or a Hoffmann. Its weakness appears to be that of placing such an idea in the annals of modern life; such a process invariably weakens these powerful imaginative ideas, and takes away from, instead of adding to, the apparent truth, and cannot fail to give an affectation to the work. True, it might add to the difficulty to imagine a different state of society, past or future, but this seems a *sine quâ non*. The story of *Frankenstein* begins with a series of letters of a young man, Robert Walton, writing to his sister, Mrs. Saville in England, from St. Petersburg, where he is about to embark on a voyage in search of the North Pole. He is bent on discovering the secret of the magnet, and is deluded with the hope of a *never* absent sun. When advanced some distance towards his longed-for goal, Walton writes of a most strange adventure which befalls them in the midst of the ice regions— a gigantic being, of human shape, being drawn over the ice in a sledge by dogs. Not many hours after this strange sight a fresh discovery was made of another man in another sledge, with only one living dog to it: this time the man was seen to be a European, whom the sailors tried to persuade to enter their ship. On seeing Walton the stranger, speaking English, asked whither they were bound before he would consent to enter the ship. This naturally caused intense excitement, as the man, reduced to a skeleton, seemed to have but a short time to live. However, on hearing that the vessel was bound northwards, he consented to enter, and with great care he was restored for the time. In answer to an inquiry as to his object in thus exposing himself, he replied, "To seek one who fled from me." An affection springs up and increases between Walton and the stranger, till the latter promises to tell his sad and strange story, which he had hitherto intended should die with him.

This commencement leads to the story being told in the form (which might with advantage have been avoided) of a long narrative by the dying man. The stranger describes himself as of a Genevese family of high distinction, and gives an interesting account of his father and juvenile surroundings, including a playfellow, Elizabeth Lavenga, whom we encounter much later in his history. All his studies are pursued with zest, till coming upon the works of Cornelius Agrippa he is led with enthusiasm into the ideas of experimental philosophy; a passing remark of "trash" from his father, who does not explain the difference between past and modern science, is not enough to deter him and prevent the fatal consequence of the study he persists in, and thus a pupil of Albertus Magnus appears in the eighteenth century. The effects of a thunderstorm, described from those Mary had recently witnessed, decided him in his resolution, for electricity now was the aim of his research. After having passed his youth in his happy Swiss home with his parents and dear friends, on the death of his loved mother he starts for the University of Ingolstadt. Here he is much reprehended by the professors for his useless studies, until one, a Mr. Waldeman, sympathises with him, and explains how Cornelius Agrippa and others, although their studies did not bring the immediate fruit they expected, nevertheless helped on science in other directions, and he advises Frankenstein to pursue his studies in natural philosophy, including mathematics. The upshot of this advice is that two years are spent in intense study and thought, till he becomes thin and haggard in appearance. He is contemplating a visit to his home, when, making some fresh experiment, he finds that he has discovered the principle of life; this so overcomes him for a time that, oblivious of all else, he is bent on making use of his discovery. After much perplexing thought he determines to create a being superior to man, so that future generations shall bless him. In the first place, by the help of chemistry, he has to construct the form which is to be animated. The grave has to be ransacked in the attempt, and Frankenstein describes with loathing some of the details of his work, and shows the danger of overstraining the mind in any one direction—how the virtuous become vicious, and how virtue itself, carried to excess, lapses into vice.

The form is created in nervous fear and fever. Frankenstein being the ideal scientist, devoid of all feeling for art (whose ideas of it, indeed, might be limited to the elevation and section of a pot), without any ideal of proportion or beauty, reaches the point where he considers nothing but the infusion of life necessary. All is ready, and in the first hour of the morning he applies his fatal discovery. Breath is given, the limbs move, the eyes open, and the colossal being or monster, as he is henceforth called, becomes animated; though copied from statues, its fearful size, its terrible complexion and drawn skin, scarcely concealing arteries and muscles beneath, add to the horror of the expression. And this is the end of two years work to the horrified Frankenstein. Overwhelmed by disgust, he can only rush from the room, and finally falls exhausted on his bed, only to wake to find his monster grinning at him. He runs forth into the street, and here, in Mary's first work, we have a reminiscence of her own infant days, when she and Claire hid themselves under the sofa to hear Coleridge read his poem, for the following stanza from the *Ancient Mariner* might seem almost the key-note of *Frankenstein*:—

Like one who on a lonely road,
  Doth walk in fear and dread,

And having once turned round, walks on,
  And turns no more his head,
Because he knows a fearful fiend
  Doth close behind him tread.

Frankenstein hurries on, but coming across his old friend Henri Clerval at the stage coach, he recalls to mind his father, Elizabeth, his former life and friends. He returns to his rooms with his friend. Reaching his door, he trembles, but opening it, finds himself delivered from his self-created fiend. His frenzy of delight being attributed to madness from overwork, Clerval induces Frankenstein to leave his studies, and, finally (after he had for months endured a terrible illness), to accompany him to his native village. Various delays occurring, they are detained too late in the year to pass the dangerous roads on their way home.

Health and peace of mind returning to some degree, Frankenstein is about to proceed on his journey homewards, when a letter arrives from his father with the fatal news of the mysterious death of his young brother. This event hastens still further his return, and gives a renewed gloomy turn to his mind; not only is his loved little brother dead, but the extraordinary event points to some unknown power. From this time Frankenstein's life is one agony. One after another all whom he loves fall victims to the demon he has created; he is never safe from his presence; in a storm on the Alps he encounters him; in the fearful murders which annihilate his family he always recognises his hand. On one occasion his creation wished to have a truce and to come to terms with his creator. This, after his most fearful treachery had caused the innocent to be sentenced as the perpetrator of his fearful deeds. On meeting Frankenstein he recounts the most pathetic story of his falling away from sympathy with humanity: how, after saving the life of a girl from drowning, he is shot by a young man who rushes up and rescues her from him. He became the unknown benefactor of a family for some period of time by doing the hard work of the household while they slept. Having taking refuge in a hovel adjoining a corner of their cottage, he hears their pathetic and romantic story, and also learns the language and ways of men; but on his wishing to make their acquaintance the family are so horrified at his appearance that the women faint, the men drive him off with blows, and the whole family leave a neigbourhood, the scene of such an apparition. After these experiences he retaliates, till meeting Frankenstein he proposes these terms: that Frankenstein shall create another being as repulsive as himself to be his companion—in fact, he desires a wife as hideous as he is. These were the conditions, and the lives of all those whom Frankenstein held most dear were in the balance; he hesitated long, but finally consented.

Everything now had to be put aside to carry out this fearful task—his love of Elizabeth, his father's entreaties that he should marry her, his hopes, his ambitions, go for nothing. To save those who remain, he must devote himself to his work. To carry out his aim he expresses a wish to visit England, and, with his friend Clerval, descends the Rhine, which is described with the knowledge gained in Mary's own journey, and the same route is pursued which she, Shelley, and Claire had taken through Holland, embarking for England from Rotterdam, and thence reaching the Thames. After passing London and Oxford and various places of interest, he expresses a desire to be left for a time in solitude, and selects a remote island of the Orkneys, where an uninhabited hut answers the purpose of his laboratory. Here he works unmolested till his fearful task is nearly accomplished, when a fear and loathing possess his soul at the possible result of this second achievement. Although the demon already created has sworn to abandon the haunts of man and to live in a desert country with his mate, what hold will there be over this second being with an individuality and will of its own? What might be the future consequences to humanity of the existence of such monsters? He forms a resolution to abandon his dreaded work, and at that moment it is confirmed by the sight of his monster grinning at him through the window of the hut in the moonlight. Not a moment is lost. He tears his just completed work limb from limb. The monster disappears in rage, only to return to threaten eternal revenge on him and his; but the time of weakness is passed; better encounter any evils that may be in store, even for those he loves, than leave a curse to humanity. From that time there is no truce. Clerval is murdered and Frankenstein is seized as the murderer, but respited for worse fate; he is married to Elizabeth, and she is strangled within a few hours. When goaded to the verge of madness by all these events, and seeing his beloved father reduced to imbecility through their misfortunes, he can make no one believe his self-accusing story; and if they did, what would it avail to pursue a being who could scale the Alps, live among glaciers, and pass unfathomable seas? There is nothing left but a pursuit till death, single-handed, when one might expire and the other be appeased—onward, with a deluding sight from time to time of his avenging demon. Only in sleep and dreams did Frankenstein find forgetfulness of his self-imposed torture, for he lived again with those he had loved; he endured life in his pursuit by imagining his waking hours to be a horrible dream and longing for the night, when sleep should bring him life. When hopes of meeting his demon failed, some fresh trace would appear to lead him on through habited and uninhabited countries; he tracks him to the verge of the eternal ice, and even there procures a sledge from the wretched and horrified inhabitants of the last dwelling-place of men to pursue the monster, who, on a similar vehicle, had departed, to their delight. Onwards, onwards, over the eternal ice they pass, the pursued and the pursuer, till consciousness is nearly lost, and Frankenstein is rescued by those to whom he now narrates his history; all except his fatal scientific secret, which is to die with him shortly, for the end cannot be far off.

The story is told; and the friend—for he feels the utmost sympathy with the tortures of Frankenstein—can only attempt to soothe his last days or hours, for he, too, feels the end must be near; but at this crisis in Frankenstein's existence the expedition cannot proceed northward, for the crew mutiny to return. Frankenstein determines to proceed alone; but his strength is ebbing, and Walton foresees his early death. But this is not to pass quietly, for the demon is in no mood that his creator should escape unmolested from his grasp. Now the time is ripe, and, during a momentary absence, Walton is startled by fearful sounds, and then, in the cabin of his dying friend, a sight to appal the bravest; for the fiend is having the death struggle with him— then all is over. Some last speeches of the demon to Walton are explanatory of his deed, and of his present intention of self-immolation, as he has now slaked his thirst to wreak vengeance for his existence. Then he disappears over the ice to accomplish this last task.

Surely there is enough weird imagination for the subject. Mary in this work not merely intended to depict the horror of such a monster, but she evidently wished also to show what a being, with no naturally bad propensities, might sink to when under the influence of a false position—the education of Rousseau's natural man not being here possible.

Some weak points, some incongruities, it would be unreasonable not to expect. Whether the *eternal* light expected at the North Pole, if of the sun, was a misapprehension of the author or a Shelleyan application of the word eternal (as applied by him to certain friendships, or duration of residence in houses) may be questioned. The question as to the form used for the narrative has already been referred to. The difficulty of such a method is strangely exemplified in the long letters which are quoted by Frankenstein to his friend while dying, and which he could not have carried with him on his deadly pursuit. Mary's facility in writing was great, and having visited some of the most interesting places in the world, with some of the most interesting people, she is saved from the dreary dulness of the dull. Her ideas, also, though sometimes affected, are genuine, not the outcome of some fashionable foible to please a passing faith or superstition, which ought never to be the *raison d'etre* of a romance, though it may be of a satire or a sermon.

The last passage in the book is perhaps the weakest. It is scarcely the climax, but an anticlimax. The end of Frankenstein is well conceived, but that of the Demon fails. It is ridiculous to conceive anyone, demon or human, having ended his vengeance, fleeing over the ice to burn himself on a funeral pyre where no fuel could be found. Surely the tortures of the lowest pit of Dante's Inferno might have sufficed for the occasion. The youth of the authoress of this remarkable romance has raised comparison between it and the first work of a still younger romancist, the author of *Gabriel Denver*, written at seventeen, who died before he had completed his twentieth year.

While this romance was being planned during the latter part of the stay of the Shelley party in Switzerland, after their return from Chamouni, the diary gives us a charming idea of their life in their cottage of Montalègre. We have the books they read, as usual; and well did Mary, no less than Shelley, make use of that happy reading-time of life—youth. The Latin authors read by Shelley were also studied by Mary. We find her reading "Quintus Curtius," ten and twelve pages at a time; also on Shelley's birthday, August 4, she reads him the fourth book of Virgil, while in a boat with him on the lake. Also the fire-balloon is not forgotten, which Mary had made two or three days in advance for the occasion. They used generally to visit Diodati in the evening, after dinner, though occasionally Shelley dined with Byron, and accompanied him in his boat. On one occasion Mary wrote: "Shelley and Claire go up to Diodati; I do not, for Lord Byron did not seem to wish it." Rousseau, Voltaire, and other authors cause the time to fly, until their spirits are damped by a letter arriving from Shelley's solicitor, requiring his return to England. While in Switzerland Mary received some letters from Fanny, her half-sister; these letters are interesting, showing a sweet, gentle disposition, very affectionate to both Shelley and Mary. One letter asks Mary questions about Lord Byron. There are also details as to the unfortunate state of the finances of Godwin, who seemed in a perennial state of needing three hundred pounds. Fanny also writes of herself, on July 29, 1816, as not being well—being in a state of mind which always keeps her body in a fever—her lonely life, after her sister's departure, with all the money anxieties, and her own dependence, evidently weighed upon her mind, and led to a state of despondency, although her letters would scarcely give the idea of a tragedy being imminent. She writes to Shelley and Mary that Mrs. Godwin—mamma she calls her—tells her that she is the laughing-stock of Mary and Shelley, and the constant "beacon of their satire." She shows much affection for little William, as well as for his parents; but there is certainly no word in these letters showing more than sisterly and friendly feeling; no word showing jealousy or envy. Claire afterwards alleged that Fanny had been in love with Shelley. Mr. Kegan Paul states the reverse most strongly. It is not easy to conceive how either should have been sure of the fact. Even Shelley's beautiful verses to her memory do not indicate any special reason for her sadness, as far as he was concerned.

Her voice did quiver as we parted,
  Yet knew I not that heart was broken
From which it came, and I departed,
  Heeding not the words then spoken.

Misery—oh Misery!
This world is all too wide for thee.

From these lines we see that Fanny was in a very depressed state of mind when her sister left England for her second Continental tour in 1816. This being two years from the time when Mary had first left her home, it does not seem probable that Shelley was to blame, or rather was the indirect cause of Fanny's sadness. She felt herself generally useless and unneeded in the world, and this idea weighed her down.

CHAPTER VIII.

RETURN TO ENGLAND.

On leaving the Lake of Geneva on August 28, without having accomplished anything in the way of a settlement for Claire, but with pleasant reminiscences of Rousseau's surroundings, and the grandeur of the Alps, the party of three returned towards England by way of Dijon, and thence by a different route from that by which they had gone, returning by Rouvray, Auxerre, Fontainebleau, and Versailles. Here Mary and Shelley visited the palace and town, which a few years hence she would revisit under far different circumstances. Travelling—in those days so very unlike what it is in ours, when Europe can be crossed without being examined—allowed them to become acquainted with the towns they passed through. Rouen was visited; but for some reason they were disappointed with the cathedral. Prom Havre they sailed for Portsmouth, when, with their usual fate, they encountered a stormy passage of twenty-seven hours. It must have been a trying journey for them in more ways than one, for if there was any uncertainty as to Claire's position on leaving England, Mary could now no longer have been in any doubt. On arriving in England she proceeded, with Claire and her little William, with his Swiss nurse Elise, to Bath, where Claire passed as Mrs. Clairemont. Shelley addressed her as such at 5 Abbey Churchyard, Bath. During this time Shelley was again house-hunting, while staying with Peacock on the banks of the Thames; and Mary paid a visit to Peacock at the same time, leaving little William to the care of Elise and Claire at Bath. From here Claire writes to Mary about the "Itty Babe's" baby ways, and how she and Elise puzzled and puzzled over the little night-gowns, or, quoting Albè, as they called Byron (it has been suggested a condensation of L. B.), "they mused and coddled" without effect. Claire certainly did her best to take care of the baby, walking out with it, and so forth.

Now the three hundred pounds written of by Fanny was falling due. Mary must also have been kept in great apprehension, as we see by a letter from Shelley to Godwin, dated October 2, 1816, that the money was not forthcoming, as hoped. So the fatal Rhine gold is again helping to a tragedy, which the romantic prefer to impute to a still more fatal cause; for, so short a time after the 2nd as October 10, we find Fanny already at Bristol, writing to Godwin that she is about to depart immediately to the place whence she hopes never to return. On October 3 there is a long letter from her to Mary, written just after Shelley's letter had reached Godwin, when she had read its contents on Godwin's countenance as he perused it. Her letter is most clear-sighted, noble, and single-minded; she complains of Mary's way of exaggerating Mrs. Godwin's resentment to herself, explaining that whatever Mrs. Godwin may say in moments of extreme irritation to her, she is quite incapable of making the worst of Mary's behaviour to others. She shows Mary her own carelessness in leaving letters about for the servants to read, so that they and Harriet spread the reports she complains of rather than Mrs. Godwin. She tells how she had tried to convince Shelley that he should only keep French servants, and she endeavours to persuade Mary how important it is that they should prevent bad news coming to Godwin in a way to give a sudden shock, as he is so sensitive. She saw through certain subterfuges of Shelley, and wrote in a calm, affectionate way, trying to set everything right, with a wonderful clearness of vision; for everyone but herself—for herself there was no outlet but despair, no rest but the grave; she, the utterly unselfish one, was useless—all that remained was to smooth her way to the grave. Not for herself, but others, she managed to die where she was unknown, travelling for this purpose to Swansea, where only a few shillings remained to her, and a little watch Mary had brought her from Geneva. She wrote of herself in a letter she left, which neither compromised anyone nor indicated who she was, as one whose birth was unfortunate, but whose existence would soon be forgotten. Poor Fanny! Is she not rather likely to be remembered as a type of self-abnegation? Certainly hers was not the nature to cause her sister a moment's jealous pang, even though her death called forth one of Shelley's sweetest lyrics.

There was nothing to be done. Godwin paid a brief visit to the scene, and ascertained that all was too true. The door that had had to be forced, the laudanum bottle, and her letter told all that need be known. Shelley visited Bristol to obtain information; but there was no use in giving publicity to this fresh family sorrow—discretion was the only sympathy that could be shown. Mary bought mourning, and worked at it. Claire envied for herself Fanny's rest; but life had to proceed, awaiting fresh events.

Work was the great resource. Mary was writing her *Frankenstein*. She persisted with the utmost fortitude in intellectual employment, as poor Fanny wrote to Mary on September 26:—"I cannot help envying your calm, contented disposition, and the calm philosophical habits of life which pursue yon; or, rather, which you pursue everywhere; I allude to your description of the manner in which you pass your days at Bath, when most women would hardly have recovered from the fatigues of such a journey as you had been taking."

This is, indeed, the key-note of Mary's character, which, with her sensitive, retiring nature, enabled her to live through the stormy times of her life with equanimity.

Mary had Shelley's company through November, but at the beginning of December she writes to Shelley, who is again staying with Peacock house-hunting. Mary tells him what she would *like*: "A house (with a lawn) near a river or lake, noble trees, or divine mountains"; but she would be content if

Shelley would give her "a garden and absentia Claire." This is very different from her way of thinking of Fanny, who, she says, might now have had a home with her. This expression occurs in a letter to Shelley when she was on the point of marrying him, and might have had Fanny with her. Mary also speaks of her drawing lessons, and how (thank God!) she had finished "that tedious, ugly picture" she had been so long about. This points to that terrible way of teaching Art, by accustoming its students to hideousness and vulgarity, till Art itself might become an unknown quantity. Mary also tells, what is more interesting, that she has finished the fourth chapter, a very long one, of her *Frankenstein*, which she thinks Shelley will like. She wishes for his return. On December 13 Mary receives a letter from Shelley, who is with Leigh Hunt. On December 15, 1816, he is back with Mary at Bath, when a letter from Hookham, who had been requested by Shelley to obtain information about Harriet for him, brought further fatal news—for Harriet had now committed suicide, and had been found drowned in the Serpentine. Unknown, she was called Harriet Smith; uncared for, she had gone to her grave beneath the water—unloved, the lovely Harriet cared not to live. What may have happened, it is not for those who may not have been tried to question; of cause and effect it is not for us to judge; but that her memory must have been a haunting shadow to Shelley and to Mary no one would wish to think them heartless enough to deny. Surely the lovely "Lines," with no name affixed, must be the dirge to Harriet's fate, and Shelley's life's failure:—

The cold earth slept below;
Above, the cold sky shone;
    And all around
    With a chilling sound,
From caves of ice and fields of snow,
The breath of night like death did flow
    Beneath the sinking moon.

The wintry hedge was black;
The green grass was not seen;
    The birds did rest
    On the bare thorn's breast,
Whose roots, beside the pathway-track,
Had bound their folds o'er many a crack
    Which the frost had made between.

Thine eyes glowed in the glare
Of the moon's dying light.
    As a fen-fire's beam
    On a sluggish stream
Gleams dimly, so the moon shone there;

And it yellowed the strings of thy tangled hair,
That shook in the wind of night.

The moon made thy lips pale, beloved;
The wind made thy bosom chill:
    The night did shed
    On thy dear head
Its frozen dew, and thou didst lie
Where the bitter breath of the naked sky
    Might visit thee at will.

These lines are dated 1815 by Mary in her edition, but she says she cannot answer for the accuracy of all the dates of minor poems.

The death of Harriet was necessarily quickly followed by the marriage of Shelley and Mary. The most sound opinions were ascertained as to the desirability of an early marriage, or of postponing the ceremony for a year after the death of Harriet; all agreed that the wedding ought to take place without delay, and it was fixed for December 30, 1816, at St. Mildred's Church in the City, where Godwin and his wife were present, to their no little satisfaction, as described by Shelley to Claire. Mary notes her marriage thus in her diary: "I have omitted writing my journal for some time. Shelley goes to London, and returns; I go with him; spend the time between Leigh Hunt's and Godwin's. A marriage takes place on the 30th December 1816. Draw. Read Lord Chesterfield and Locke."

No sooner was the marriage over than their one anxiety was to return to Bath; for now the time of Claire's trial was approaching, and on January 13 a little girl was born, not destined to remain long in a world so sad for some. Little Allegra, a child of rare beauty, was welcomed by Shelley and Mary with all the benevolence they were capable of, and Byron's duty to his child devolved, for the time at least, on Shelley.

During this period, Shelley's and Mary's chief anxiety was to welcome and care for the little children left by poor Harriet. They had been placed, before her death, under the care of a clergyman who kept a school in Warwick, the Rev. John Kendall, vicar of Budbrooke. Shelley had hoped that his marriage with Mary would remove all difficulty, and Mary was waiting to welcome Ianthe and Charles; but in this matter they were doomed to disappointment.

On January 8 a Bill was filed in the Court of Chancery, on the part of the infants Charles and Ianthe Shelley, John Westbrook, their maternal grandfather, acting on their behalf, praying that they might not be transferred to the care of their father, Percy Bysshe Shelley, who had deserted their mother; who was the author of *Queen Mab*, and an avowed atheist, who wrote against the institution of marriage, and who had been living unlawfully with a woman whom Eliza Westbrook (as Shelley had written to her) might excusably regard as the cause of her sister's ruin. Shelley filed his answer on the 18th, denying the desertion of his wife, as she and he had separated with mutual consent, owing to various causes. He had wished for his children on parting with her, but left them with her at her urgent entreaty. He had given her two hundred pounds to pay her debts, and an allowance of a fifth of his income. As to his theological opinions, he understands that they are abandoned as not applicable to the case. His views on matrimony, he alleged, were only in accordance with the ideas of some of the greatest thinkers that divorce ought to be possible under various conditions.

Lord Eldon gave his judgment on March 27, 1817. In fifteen carefully worded paragraphs he showed his reasons for depriving Shelley of his children. He insists through all that it is Shelley's avowed and published opinions, as they affected his *conduct* in life, which unfitted him to be the guardian of his children.

The wording in some passages caused grave anxiety to Shelley and Mary (as shown in their letters) as to whether they would be deprived of their own children; and they were prepared to abandon everything, property, country, all, and to escape with the infants. The poem "To William" was written under this misapprehension, although when he left England in 1818, Shelley's chief reason, as given in his letter to Godwin, was on account of his health. Undoubtedly the judgment, and all the trying circumstances they had been passing through ever since their return from Geneva, helped to decide them in this determination.

Charles and Ianthe were finally placed under the care of Dr. and Mrs. Hume, who were to receive two hundred pounds a year—eighty pounds settled on them by Westbrook, and one hundred and twenty pounds to be paid by Shelley for the charge. Shelley might see them twelve times a year in the presence of the Humes, the Westbrooks twelve times alone, and Sir Timothy and his family when they chose.

While these proceedings were progressing, Mary with Claire and the two children had moved to Marlow, having previously joined Shelley in London on January 26, as she feared to leave him in his depressed state alone. The intellectual society they met at Hunt's and at Godwin's helped to pass over this trying period. One evening Mary saw together the "three poets"—Hunt, Shelley, and Keats; Keats not being much drawn towards Shelley, while Hazlitt, who was also present, was unfavourably impressed by his worn and sickly appearance, induced by the terrible anxieties and trials which be had recently passed through. Horace Smith also proved a staunch friend: Shelley once remarked it was odd that the only truly generous wealthy person he ever met should be a stockbroker, and that he should write and care for poetry, and yet make money. In the midst of her anxieties, Mary Shelley enjoyed more social intercourse and amusement than before. We find her noting in her diary, in February, dining with the Hunts and Horace Smith, going to the opera of *Figaro*, music, &c. But now they had found their Marlow retreat—a house with a garden as Mary desired, not with a river view, but a shady little orchard, a kitchen garden, yews, cypresses, and a cedar tree. Here Mary was able to live unsaddened for a time; the Swiss nurse for the children, a cook and man-servant, sufficed for in-door and out-door work, and Mary, true to her name, was able to occupy herself with spiritual and intellectual employment, not to the neglect of domestic, as the succession of visitors entertained must prove; study, drawing, and her beloved work of *Frankenstein* were making rapid progress. Nor could Mary have been indifferent to the woes of the poor, for Shelley would scarcely have been so actively benevolent as recorded during the residence at Marlow without the co-operation of his wife. While Shelley enquired into cases of distress and gave written orders for money, Mary dispensed the latter. Here Godwin paid them his first visit, and the Hunts passed a pleasant time. Shelley wrote his *Revolt of Islam* under the Bisham Beeches, and Mary had the pleasure of welcoming her old friend Mr. Baxter, of Dundee, although his daughter Isabel, married to Mr. Booth, still held aloof. Peacock, Horace Smith, and Hogg were also among the guests. We find constant references to Godwin having been irritated and querulous with Mary or Shelley. A forced, unnatural, equanimity during one period of his life seems to have resulted in a querulous irritability later—a not unusual case—and he had to vent it on those who loved and revered him most, or in fact, on those who would alone endure it from amiability of disposition, a quality not remarkable in his second wife.

On May 14 we find Mary has finished and corrected her *Frankenstein*, and she decides to go to London and stay with her father while carrying on the negotiations with Murray whom she wishes to publish it. Shelley accompanies Mary for a few days at Godwin's invitation, but returns to look after "Blue Eyes," to whom he is charged with a million kisses from Mary. But Mary returns speedily to Shelley and "Blue Eyes," having felt very restless while absent. She soon falls into a plan of Shelley's for partially adopting a little Polly who frequently spent the day or slept in their house, and Mary would find time to tell her before she went to bed whatever she or Shelley had been reading that day, always asking her what she thought of it.

Mary, who was expecting another child in the autumn, was not long idle after the completion of *Frankenstein*, but set to work copying and revising her *Six Weeks' Tour*. This work, begun in August, she completed after the birth of her baby Clara on September 2. In October the book was bought and published by Hookham.

She tells, in her notes on this year 1817, how she felt the illness and sorrows which Shelley passed through had widened his intellect, and how it was the source of some of his noblest poems, but that he had lost his early dreams of changing the world by an idea, or, at least, he no longer expected to see the result.

A letter from Mary to her husband, written soon after the birth of her baby, shows how anxious she was at that time about his health. It had been a positive pain to her to see him languid and ill, and she counselled him obtaining the best advice. Change being recommended by the physician, Mary has to decide between going to the seaside or Italy. With all the reasons for and against Italy, Mary asks Shelley to let her know distinctly his wish in the matter, as she can be well anywhere. One strong reason for their going to Italy is that Alba, as Allegra was then called, should join her father. Evidently the embarrassment was too great to settle how to account for the poor child longer in England; and had not she a just claim upon Byron?

In another letter, September 28, Mary speaks of Claire's return to Marlow in a croaking state—everything wrong; Harriet's debts enormous. She had just been out for her first walk after the birth of Clara, and was surprised to find how much warmer it was out than in. Shelley is commissioned to buy a seal-skin fur hat for Willy, and to take care that it is a round fashionable shape for a boy. She is surrounded by babies while writing—William, Alba, and little Clara. Her love is to be given to Godwin when Mrs. Godwin is not there, as she does not love her. *Frankenstein* is still undisposed of.

The house at Marlow is soon found to be far too cold for a winter residence. Italy or the sea must speedily be settled on. Alba is the great consideration in favour of Italy, Mary feels she will not be safe except with them; Byron is so difficult to fix in any way, and the one hope seems to be to get him to provide for the child. Anxiety for Alba's future ruled their present, so impossible is it to foretell the future, which, read and judged as our past, is easy to be severe upon. This dream of health and rest in Italy was not to be so easily realised. Instead of being there, they were still dispensing charity at Marlow at the end of December, in spite of various negotiations for money in October and November. Horace Smith had lent two hundred pounds, and, Shelley thought, would lend more. Mary continued extremely anxious on Alba's account. If she could only be got to her father! Who could tell how he might change his mind if there be much delay? Might he not "change his mind, or go to Greece, or to the devil; and then what happens?" The lawyers' delays were heavy trials, and they could not go and leave Godwin unprovided for; he was a great anxiety to Mary at this time. It was not till December 7 that Shelley wrote to tell Godwin how he felt bound to go to Italy, as he had been informed that he was in a consumption.

Owing to a visit of Mr. Baxter to them at Marlow, when he wrote a most enthusiastic letter about Shelley and Mary to his daughter Isabel Booth, Mary had hoped for a renewal of the friendship which had afforded her so much pleasure as a girl, and she invited Isabel to accompany them to Italy; but this Mr. Booth would not allow, and, in fact, he appears to have treated his father-in-law, Mr. Baxter, who was six years younger than himself, with much severity, and wished him to stop all intimacy with Shelley. He did not, however, prevent him having a friendly parting with Shelley on March 2, although he would not allow his wife to have any communication with Mary—much to their sorrow. Mary was in constant anxiety about Shelley in the last months of 1817, writing of his suffering and the distress she feels in seeing him in such pain and looking so ill. In January 1818, the month before they left Marlow, his sufferings became very great. But two thousand pounds being borrowed on the promise of four thousand five hundred pounds on his father's death, and the house at Marlow being sold on January 25th, we find the packing and flitting taking place soon after. By February 7, Shelley leaves for London, and on Tuesday 10th Mary follows. Godwin, as usual now, had been beseeching for money, and then, feeling his dignity wounded by the effort, retaliated on the giver with haughtiness and insulting demands. In a biography, unfortunately, characters cannot always be made the consistent beings they frequently become in romances.

One more happy month Mary is to pass in England with Shelley. We, again, have accounts of visits to the opera, to museums, plays, dinners, and pleasant evenings spent with friends. Keats is again met, and Shelley calls on Mr. Baxter, who is not allowed by his son-in-law to say farewell to Mary Shelley: such a martinet may a Scotch schoolmaster be. Mary Lamb calls, and visits are paid and received till the last evening arrives, when Shelley, exhausted with ill-health, fatigue, and excitement, fell into one of his profound sleeps on the sofa before some of his friends left the lodgings in Great Russell Street, and thus the Hunts were unable to exchange with him their farewells. This small band of literary friends were all to bid Shelley and Mary farewell on his last few days in England. The contrast is indeed marked between that time and this, when Shelley societies are found in various parts of the world, when enthusiasts write from the most remote regions and form friendships in his name, when, churches, including Westminster Abbey, have rung in praise of his ideal yearnings, and when, not least, some have certainly tried to lead pure unselfish lives in memory of the godlike part of the man in him; but he now left his native shores, never to return, with Claire and Allegra, and his own two little children, and certainly a true wife willing to follow him through weal or woe.

CHAPTER IX.

LIFE IN ITALY.

A third time, on March 11, 1818, Shelley, Mary, and Claire are on the road to Dover, this time with three young lives to care for—Willie, aged two years and two months; Clara, six months; and Allegra, one year and two months. These small beings kept well during their journey, and it is touching to note how Claire Clairmont, in her part of the diary recording their progress, mentions bathing her darling at Dover, and then cancels the passage from her diary, as many others where her name is given—surely one of the saddest of things for a mother to fear to mention her child's name! After another stormy passage the party again reached Calais, which they found as delightful as ever, and where they stayed at the Grand Cerf Hotel.

Mary continues to note the journey. They took a different route this time—by Douai, La Fère, Rheims, Berri-le-bac, and St. Dizier, the road winding by the Marne. They sleep at Langres, which ramparted town surely ought to have left a pleasant reminiscence; but they had hitherto found the route uninteresting and fatiguing. Mary finds more interest in the country after Langres, and with the help of Schlegel, from whom Shelley read out loud to her, the time passed pleasantly; no long weary evenings in hotels; no complaints when a carriage broke down and they were kept three hours at Macon for it to be repaired: they had with them the friends of whom they never tired.

At Lyons they rested three days. Mary much admired the city, and they visited the theatre, where they saw *L'homme gris et le Physionomiste*; and on Wednesday, March 25, they set out towards the mountains whose white tops were seen at a distance.

In crossing the frontier there was a difficulty in getting their books allowed to enter Sardinian territory, until a Canon, who had met Shelley's father at the Duke of Norfolk's, helped to get them through. After leaving Chambéry, where Mary stayed to allow her nurse Elise to see her child, they crossed Mont Cenis and dined on the top. The beauty of the scenery greatly raised Shelley's spirits, causing him to sing with exultation. They stayed one night at Turin, visiting the opera; and after reaching Milan, Shelley and Mary went to Lake Como for a few days, having some idea of spending the summer on its banks; but not being able to suit themselves with a house they returned to Milan on April 12 and rejoined Claire, who had remained with the children. During the stay at Milan till the end of April there had been frequent letters from Claire to Byron. These were evidently far from satisfactory, as we find Shelley writing letters of caution to Claire in 1822, with regard to Byron and Allegra: he mentions having warned her against letting Byron get possession of Allegra in the spring of 1818, but Claire thought it for the interest of the child, whom she undoubtedly loved, to let her go to her father. Walks in the public gardens with the "Chicks" are noted by Claire several times, and the last entry in her diary, before April 28, when Allegra was taken by the nurse Elise to Byron, mentions a walk with the "Chicks" in the morning and drive in the evening with them, Mary and Shelley. Mary had sent her own trusted nurse Elise with the little Allegra, feeling that she would remain and in some degree replace the mother; and Claire believed that the child would stay with its father, though certainly this did not seem desirable or likely to last for long.

A change of scene being needed after these trying emotions, Mary, with her husband and two children, and Claire, now left for Pisa and Leghorn. They slept on the way at Piacenza, Parma, Modena, and then passed a night at a little inn among the Apennines, the fifth at Barberino, the sixth at La Scala, and on the seventh reached Pisa, where they lodged at Le Tre Donzelle. On this journey Mary was able to enjoy the Italian scenery under the unclouded Italian sky—the vine-festooned trees amid the fields of corn, the hedges full of flowers; all these seen from the carriage convey a lasting impression, and poor Claire remarks that, driving in a long, straight road, she always hopes it will take her to some place where she will be happier. They pass through beautiful chestnut woods on the southern side of the Apennines, and along the fertile banks of the Arno to Pisa. After a few days' stay at Pisa, where the cathedral, "loaded with pictures and ornaments," and the leaning tower are visited, and where, perhaps, the quiet Campo Santo, with its chapel covered with the beautiful frescos of Orcagna and Gozzoli, &c., was enjoyed, they proceed to Leghorn; here, after a few days at L'Aquila Nera, they move into apartments. They meet and see much of Mary's mother's friend, Mrs. Gisborne, who grew much attached to both Shelley and Mary, and who, from her acquaintance with literary people, must have been a pleasant companion to them. They had letters of introduction to the Gisbornes from Godwin. While here Mary made progress with Italian, reading Ariosto with her husband. Leghorn was not a sufficiently interesting place to detain the wandering Shelleys long, in spite of the attractions of the Gisbornes. On June 11 Mary, with her two children and Claire, follows Shelley to Bagni di Lucca, where he had taken a house. Here Mary much enjoyed the quiet after noisy Leghorn, as she wrote to Mrs. Gisborne, hoping to attract her to visit them. Mary was in her element in shady woods within the sound of running waters; her only annoyance was the number of English she came in contact with in her walks, where the English nursery-maid flourished, "a kind of animal I by no means like" she wrote; neither was she pleased by "the dashing, staring Englishwomen, who surprise the Italians (who always are carried about in sedan chairs) by riding on horseback."

Mary and Claire used to visit the Casino with Shelley, and look on at the dancing in which they did not join. Mary, however, did not agree with Shelley in admiring the Italian style of dancing; but those things on which they were ever of the same mind they had in plenty, for their beloved books arrived after being scrutinised by the Church authority; and while Shelley revelled in the delights of Greek literature, Mary shared those of English with him, for who can estimate the advantage of hearing Shakespeare and other poets read by Shelley! It was at the baths of Lucca also that Mary found her husband's unfinished *Rosalind and Helen*, and prevailed on him to complete it, for, as she says in her notes, "Shelley had no care for any of his poems that did not emanate from the depths of his mind and develop some high or abstruse truth." Without doubt, Mary was the ideal wife for Shelley. At this stage in the career of the poet one can but deplore that relentless destiny should only bring Mary to Shelley when a victim had already been sacrificed on the altar of fate; and the more one realises the sympathetic and intellectual nature of Claire, the less possible is it to help wasting a regret that Byron could not have met with the philosopher bookseller's adopted daughter earlier, instead of ruining his nature and his life by the fashionable follies he tampered with. But who would alter the workings of destiny? Does not the finest Lacryma Christi grow on the once devastated slopes of Vesuvius? Life, too, has its earthquakes, and the eruptions of its hidden depths seen through the minds of its poets, though causing at times agony to those who come in contact with them, work surely for the good of the whole. Mary had the years of pleasure, which are inestimable to those who can appreciate them, of contact with a great mind; but few among poets' wives have had the gifts which allow them fully to participate in such pleasures. Well for Mary that she also inherited much of her father's philosophic nature, which enabled her to endure some of the trials inherent in her position. What Shelley wrote Mary would transcribe—no mere task for her—for did she not, through Shelley, enjoy Plato's *Symposium*, a translation of which he was employed upon at Lucca? How could the fashionable idlers at the Baths find time to drink in inspiration from the poet and his wife? The poet gives the depths of his nature, but it is not he who writes with the fever or the tear of emotion who can stoop to be his own interpreter to the uninitiated, which seems to be a necessity of modern times, with few exceptions. Mary's education, defective though it may have been in some details, made her a fitting companion for some of the greatest of her day, and this quality in a woman could scarcely exist without a refinement of manner and tastes which, at times, might be misleading as to her disposition.

The spirit of wandering now came over Claire, and by the middle of August her desire to see her child again could no longer be suppressed. Accordingly she set out with Shelley on August 19, and reached Florence the next day, when Shelley wrote to Mary the impression the lovely city made on him, begging her, at the same time, not to let little William forget him before his return—little Clara could not remember. Claire thought at one time of remaining at Padua, but on reaching that city could not endure being left alone, and they reached Venice in the middle of the night, during a violent storm, which Shelley did not fail to write an account of to his wife. He also told her how the Hoppners, whom they called on (Mr. Hoppner being the British Consul in Venice), advised them to act with regard to Byron. By their advice Shelley called alone on him, and Byron proposed to send Allegra to Padua for a week on a visit; he would not like her to remain longer, as the Venetians would think he had grown tired of her. He afterwards offered them his villa at Este, thinking they were all at Padua. Shelley accepted this proposal, and wrote requesting Mary to join him there with the children, not knowing whether he was acting for good or harm, but looking forward to be scolded if he had done wrong, or kissed if right—the event would prove. The event did prove; but it was out of their power to rule it.

Mary had invited the Gisbornes to stay with her at the Baths. They arrived on August 25, but the circumstances seemed imperative for Mary to go to Este, and she left on the 31st with a servant, Paolo, as attendant. They were detained a day at Florence, and did not reach Este till poor little Clara was dangerously ill from dysentery, which reduced her to a state of fever and weakness. Mary endured the misery of an incompetent doctor at Este; neither had they confidence in the Paduan physician. Shelley proceeded to Venice to obtain further advice, and prepare for the arrival of his wife and child, writing from there that he felt somewhat uneasy, but trusted there was no cause for real anxiety. This arrangement made, Mary set out with her baby and Claire to meet Shelley at Padua, and then proceeded to Venice, Claire returning to mind William and Allegra at Este; and now Mary had to endure that terrible tension of mind, with her dying child in her arms, driving to Venice, the time remembered by her so well when, on the same route, nearly a quarter of a century later, each turn in the road and the very trees seemed as the most familiar objects of her daily life; for had they not been impressed on her mental vision by the strength of despair? The Austrian soldiers at the frontier could not detain them, though without passports, for even they would not prevent a dying child from being conveyed on a forlorn hope. Such grief could scarcely be rendered more or less acute by circumstances. They arrived at their inn in a gondola, but only for Clara to die in her mother's arms within an hour.

In this trial the Hoppners proved most kind friends, taking Mary to their house, and relieving the first hopelessness of grief by kindness, which it seemed ingratitude not to respond to. Mary, whatever she may have felt, knew that no expression of her feelings in her diary would nerve her to endure. She went about her daily occupations as usual. One idle day elapsed, after her little Clara had been buried on the Lido; we find her as usual reading, shopping, and seeing Byron, with whom she hoped to make better terms for Claire with regard to Allegra. There is a curious passage in a letter from Godwin to his daughter, illustrative of his own turn of mind, and not without some general truth:—"We seldom indulge long in depression and mourning except when we think secretly that there is something very refined in it, and that it does us honour."

On September 29, Shelley and Mary return to Este. Claire had taken the children to Padua, but returned the next day to the Villa I Cappuccini. In the evening they went to the Opera. Their house was most beautifully situated. Here Shelley wrote his "Lines among the Euganean Hills," for no intense feeling could come to the poet without the necessity of expressing himself in poetry; and it was during this September month that Shelley wrote the first act of his *Prometheus Unbound*. Mary revisited Venice with her husband, little William, and the nurse Elise, on October 12. The impression then formed of Byron and his surroundings was so painful as to render it a matter of surprise that they could think of returning Allegra to him; but her extreme youth was her safeguard in this respect, and Shelley returned to Este on September 24, to take Allegra a second time from her mother who, with all her love for her "darling," as she always wrote of her in the effaced passages of her diary, could not get over the insuperable difficulties of her birth. On January 22 of this same year Claire had entered in her diary the fact of its being Byron's (Albé's) birthday; a note carefully effaced soon after. Shelley and Mary having decided to spend the winter further south, after a few days of preparation they left Este on November 5, and spent the night at Ferrara, where they visited the relics of Ariosto and Tasso, and the dungeon where the latter was incarcerated. Thence to Bologna, where they endured much fatigue in the picture galleries, poor Shelley being obliged to confess he did not pretend to taste. From Bologna, by Faenza and Cesena, they followed the coast from Rimmi to Fano, and passed an uncomfortable night at an inn at Fossombrone among the Apennines. Mary was greatly impressed by the beauty and grandeur of Spoleto. The impressive falls at Terni are duly chronicled by her; and November 19 and 20 are spent in winding through the Apennines, and then crossing the solitude of the Roman Campagna, and then Rome is reached.

In Italy, where wonder succeeds wonder, and where no place is a mere repetition of another, Mary may well have been impressed by her first visit to the Eternal City. Here, in November, she was able to sit and sketch in the Coliseum with her child and her husband, who found the wonderful ruin a source of inspiration. But Rome was now only a resting-place on their road to still sunnier Naples; and on November 27 Shelley set out a day in advance of Mary and her child to secure rooms in Naples, where Mary arrived on

December 1. In the best part of the city, facing the royal gardens in front of the marvellous bay, with Shelley for her guide, who himself made use of Madame de Staël's *Corinne* as a handbook, Livy for the antiquities, and Winckelmann for art, Mary could enjoy the sights of Naples as no ordinary sightseer would. December was devoted to expeditions—Baiæ, Vesuvius, and Pompeii. The day at Baiæ was perhaps the most delightful, with the return by moonlight in the boat to Naples. Vesuvius, with its stupendous spectacle as of heaven and hell made visible, naturally produced a profound impression, but it was a very tiring expedition, as apparently it was only Claire who had a *chaise à porteurs* for the ascent of the cone; Mary and Shelley rode on mules as far as they could go, and Claire was carried all the way in a chair—though this seems scarcely possible—from Resina. How Mary could walk through the cinders up the cone seems incomprehensible. She must have had great strength, as it is a trying task for a man, and no wonder Shelley, in spite of his pedestrian strength, was exhausted when they arrived at the hermitage of San Salvador. The winter at Naples seems to have been a trying one to Mary, in spite of sunshine and the beauties of Nature; for Shelley was in a state of depression, as is exemplified in the "Stanzas written in dejection near Naples." What the immediate cause of this was cannot be said; it seems to be one of the mysteries, or perhaps rather the one mystery, of Shelley's life. He asserted to Medwin that a lady, young, married, and of noble connections, had become infatuated with him, and declared her love of him on the eve of his departure for the Continent in 1816; that he had gently but firmly repulsed her; that she arrived in Naples on the day he did, and had soon afterwards died. It is suggested that a little girl who was left under his guardianship in Naples, and whom he spoke of as his poor Neapolitan, might possibly be the child of this lady; others doubt the story altogether, which is not to be wondered at, although nothing can be declared impossible in a life where truth is frequently so much stranger than romance.

Mary was also troubled while at Naples by her servants, an unusual subject with her; but Paolo, having gone far beyond the limits of cheating, was detected by Mary, and also obliged by her to marry Elise, whom he had betrayed. They left for Rome, but Paolo declared he would be revenged on the Shelleys, and wrote threatening letters, which a lawyer disposed of for a time. This is known to be the origin of later calumnies, which Mr. Jeaffreson has now carefully and finally refuted.

Mary, later, with the regret of love that would be all sufficient, wished that at Naples she had entered more into the cause of the grief, which Shelley had kept from her, in order not to add to the melancholy she was then feeling with regard to her father.

Before leaving Naples they succeeded in visiting the Greek ruins at Paestum, which give still a fresh impression in Italy; and then, on

February 28, 1819, Mary takes leave of Naples, never to revisit it with any of her companions of that time.

In Rome they found rooms in the Villa Parigi, but removed from them to the Palazzo Verospi on the Corso, and we soon find them busy exploring the treasures of Rome the inexhaustible. Here they had not to take fatiguing journeys as in Naples to visit the chief points of interest, for they were to be found at every turn. Visits to St. Peter's and the museum of the Vatican are mentioned; walks with Shelley to the Forum, the Capitol, and the Coliseum, which is visited and re-visited. Frequent visits are paid in the evening to the Signora Marianna Dionigi, and with her they hear Mass in St. Peter's, where the poor old Pope Pius VII was nearly dying. The Palazzo Doria and its picture gallery are examined, where the landscapes of Claude Lorraine particularly strike them. Then to the baths of Caracalla, where the romantic beauty of the ruins forms one of their chief attractions in Rome. They also take walks and drives in the Borghese Gardens. The statue of Pompey, at the base of which Cæsar fell, is not passed over—but it would be impossible to tell of all they saw and enjoyed in Rome. Mary made more acquaintances in Rome, nor did the English altogether neglect to call on Shelley. Mary also recommenced lessons in drawing, while Claire had singing lessons, and they met some celebrities at the Signora Dionigi's conversazioni. Altogether this early part of their stay in Rome was happy, but Shelley's health always fluctuating made them contemplate taking a house for the summer at Castellamare, as a doctor recommended this for him. But the days were hurrying towards a fresh calamity, for little William now fell ill, and we find the visits of a physician, Dr. Bell, chronicled, and on June 2nd three visits are noted. Claire helps to her utmost; Shelley does not close his eyes for sixty hours, and Mary, the hopes of whose life were bound up with the child, could only endure, watch the wasting of fever, and see the last of three perish on "Monday, June 7th, at noonday," as Claire enters in her diary. Mary and Shelley were deprived of their gentle, blue-eyed darling, by a stronger hand than that of the Court of Chancery, and little William was buried where Shelley was soon to follow, in the cemetery which "might make one in love with death."

CHAPTER X.

MARY'S DESPONDENCY AND BIRTH OF A SON.

Before the fatal illness of her child Willie, Mary had encountered an old friend in Rome, and had renewed her acquaintance with Miss Curran whom she had formerly known at her father's. Congenial tastes in drawing and painting drew these ladies together, and Miss Curran did or began portraits of Mary, Shelley, and, what was of more importance to them at the time, of little Willie. The portraits of Mary and of Shelley, unfinished, and by an amateur, are by no means satisfactory; certainly not giving in Mary's case an idea of the beauty and charm which are constantly referred to by her friends, and which seem to have endured up to the time when, much later, an attack of small-pox altered her appearance. The portrait of Mary, although not artistic, is interesting as painted from life. Her oval face is here given with the high forehead. The complexion described as delicate and white was not in the gift of Miss Curran, who was not a colourist. To depict the eyes grey, tending to brown near the iris, agrees with Shelley's, "brown" and Trelawny's "grey" eyes, but the beauty of expression is wanting. The mouth, thin and hard, might have caught a passing look, but certainly not what an artist would have wished to portray; while a certain stiffness of pose is not what one would expect in the high-strung, sensitive Mary Shelley. The beauty of gold-brown hair was not in the painter's power to catch. Mary was of middle height, tending towards short; her hands were considered very beautiful, and by some she was supposed to be given to displaying them, although concealing them would have been difficult and unnecessary. Her arms and neck were also beautiful. Leigh Hunt refers to her at the opera, *décolletée*, with white, gleaming, sloping shoulders. Her "voice the sweetest ever heard," added to her gifts of conversation, described as resembling her father's with an added softness of manner and charm of description, with elegance and correctness, devoid of reserve or affectation. Cyrus Redding, who much admired and esteemed her, obtained her opinion about Miss Curran's portrait of her husband, for his article in the Galignani edition of Shelley. She considered it by no means a good one, as unfinished, but with some striking points of resemblance. She consented to superintend the engraving from it for Galignani's volume, which was regarded as far more successful. Miss Curran kindly assisted with advice.

While these portraits were being executed Mary was gaining the sympathy of the painter, a boon soon much needed, for after the death of her third child her courage for a while broke down entirely. In a very delicate state of health at the time, she could not rouse herself to think of anything but her losses. With no other child needing her care, she could only abandon herself to inconsolable grief. Shelley felt that he was out of her life for the first time;

that her heart was in Rome in the grave with her child. They revisited the Falls of Terni, but the spirit had fled from the waters. They pass through bustling Leghorn, and visit the Gisbornes, but the noise is intolerable, and Shelley, ever attentive in such matters, finds a house at a short distance in the country, the Villa Valsovano, down a quiet lane surrounded by a market garden. Olives, fig trees, peach trees, myrtles, alive at night with fire-flies, must have been soothing surroundings to the wounded Mary, to whom nature was ever a kind friend. Nor were they in solitude, for they were within visiting distance of friends at Leghorn.

Two months after her loss she recommences her diary on Shelley's birthday, this time not without a wail. She writes to Mrs. Hunt of the tears she constantly sheds, and confesses she has done little work since coming to Italy. She had read, however, several books of Livy, Antenor, Clarissa, some novels, the Bible, Lucan's Pharsalia, and Dante. Shelley is reading her *Paradise Lost*, and he is writing the *Cenci*, where

That fair, blue-eyed boy,
Who was the lodestar of your life,

Mary tells us refers to William. Shelley wrote that their house was a melancholy one, and only cheered by letters from England.

On September 18 Mary wrote to her friend, Miss Curran, that they were about to move, she knew not whither. Then Shelley, with Charles Clairmont, went to Florence and engaged rooms for six months, and at the end of September Shelley returned and took his wife by slow and easy stages to the Tuscan capital, for her health was then in a very delicate state for travelling. There, in the lovely city of Florence, on November 12, 1819, she gave birth to her son Percy Florence, who first broke the spell of unhappiness which had hung for the last five months like a cloud over them; he, as events proved, was to be her one comfort with her memories, when the supreme calamity of her life fell on her, and he was mercifully spared to be the solace of her later years.

CHAPTER XI.

GODWIN AND "VALPERGA."

At this time while political events were absorbing England, and Shelley was weaving them into poetry in Italy during the remainder of his residence in Florence, Godwin's personal difficulties were reaching their climax. When he lost, in an action for the rent of his house, Shelley came to his help, but in some way Godwin expected more than he received, and became very unpleasant in his correspondence, so much so that Shelley had to beg him not to write to Mary on these subjects, as her health was not then, in October 1819, able to bear the strain, and the subject of money was not a fitting one to be pressed on her by him. Mary had not the disposal of money; if she had she would give it all to her father. He assured Godwin that the four or five thousand pounds already expended on him might have made him comfortable for the remainder of his life. Mrs. Godwin, naturally, would not hear of abandoning the Skinner Street business, as being the only provision for herself when Godwin should die. It is extremely painful at this stage of Godwin's career to witness the lowering effects of his wife's smaller nature upon him, as he certainly allowed himself to be unduly influenced by her excited and not always truthful views, as known since the early days of their married life. We have Mrs. Gisborne's diary showing how Mrs. Godwin could not endure to see anyone in 1820 who had an attachment for Mary, whom (as Godwin told Mrs. Gisborne) she considered her greatest enemy; and although he described his wife as of "the most irritable disposition possible," he listened to, and repeated her conjectures to the disparagement of Shelley and Mary at the time when she did not hesitate to accept with her husband the large sums of money which Shelley with difficulty raised for them. All the facts shown in this diary prove that Mary and Fanny must have had a sufficiently trying life at home to account for the result in either case, especially when we consider that Claire and her brother Charles both preferred to leave Godwin's house on the first possible occasion, Charles having left for France immediately after Mary's and Claire's departure with Shelley. William alone remained at home, but four years passed in a boarding school at Greenwich, from 1814, must have helped him to endure the discomforts of the time. Before Mrs. Gisborne's return to Italy Godwin gave her a detailed account, in writing, of his money transactions with Shelley, which had become very painful to both. In January, 1820, Florence proving unsuitable for Shelley's health, they left for Pisa, the mild climate of which city made it a favourite resort of the poet during most of the short remainder of his life. Mary, ever hospitable, although, as Shelley said, the bills for printing his poems must be paid for by stinting himself in meat and drink, hoped that Mrs. Gisborne would have stayed with them during her husband's visit to England in 1820, as they had moved into a pleasant apartment in March. This idea was not carried out. About this time Mary and Claire, both with their own absorbing anxieties, became again irksome to each other. Mary found relief when Claire was absent, and Claire notes how "the Claire and the Mai find something to fight about every day," a way of putting it which indicates differences, but certainly no grave cause of disturbance. This was after their removal to Leghorn, where they went towards the end of June to be near the lawyer on account of Paolo. At the beginning of August the heat at Leghorn caused the Shelleys to migrate to the baths of San Giuliano, where Shelley found a very pleasant house, Casa Prini. The moderate rent suited their slender purse, which had so many outside calls upon it.

In October Claire's departure for Florence, as governess in the family of Professor Bojti, where she went by the advice of her friend Mrs. Mason, formerly Lady Mountcashell, brought an end to her permanent residence with the Shelleys, although she was still to look upon their house as her home, and she visited them either for her pleasure or to assist them. Her absence from her friends gives us the advantage of letters from them, letters full of a certain exaggeration of affection and sympathy from Shelley, who felt more acutely than Mary that Claire might be unhappy under a strange roof. Mary, less anxious on those grounds, writes about the operas she has seen, giving good descriptions of them. One of her letters is full of anxiety as to Allegra, who has been placed in the convent of Bagnacavallo by Byron. She feels that the child ought, as soon as possible, to be taken out of the hands of so "remorseless and unprincipled a man"; but advises caution and waiting for a favourable opportunity. She hopes that he may be returning to England. "He may be reconciled with his wife." At any rate, Bagnacavallo is high and in a healthy position, quite different from the dirty canals of Venice, which might injure any child's health. Mary thus tries to console Claire, who is planning, in her imagination, various ways of getting at her child, and corresponding with and seeing Shelley on the subject. Mary dissuades Claire from attempting anything in the spring—their unlucky time. It was in the second spring Claire met L. B., &c.; the third they went to Marlow—no wise thing, at least; the fourth, uncomfortable in London; fifth, their Roman misery; the sixth, Paolo at Pisa; the seventh, a mixture of Emilia and a Chancery suit. Mary acknowledges this superstitious feeling is more in Claire's line than her own, but thinks it worth considering; but this letter to Claire carries us a year in advance.

During the summer of 1820 Mary had some of the delightful times she loved so dearly, of poetic wanderings with Shelley through woods and by the river, one of which she remembers long afterwards, when, making her note to the "Skylark," she recalls how she and Shelley, wandering through the lanes whose myrtle hedges were the bowers of the firefly, heard the carolling of the skylark which inspired one of the most beautiful of his poems. Precious memories which helped her through many after years devoid of the sympathy she yearned for. At the Baths they had the pleasure of a visit from Medwin, who gave a description of how Shelley, his wife and child, had to escape from the upper windows of their house in a boat when the canal overflowed and inundated the valley. Mary speaks of it as a very picturesque sight, with the herdsmen driving their cattle.

During the short absence of Shelley, when he took Claire to Florence, Mary was occupied planning her novel of *Valperga*, for which she studied Villani's chronicle and Sismondi's history.

On leaving the baths of San Giuliano, after the floods, the Shelleys returned to Pisa, where they passed the late autumn and winter of 1820 and the spring of 1821. Here they made more acquaintances than heretofore, Professor Pacchiani, called also "Il Diavolo," introducing them to the Prince Mavrocordato, the Princess Aigiropoli, the *improvisatore* Sgricci, Taafe, and last, not least, to Emilia Viviani. Here Mary continued to write *Valperga*, and pursued her Latin, Spanish, and Greek studies; the latter the Prince Mavrocordato assisted her with, as Mary writes to Mrs. Gisborne: "Do not you envy me my luck? that, having begun Greek, an amiable, young, agreeable, and learned Greek prince comes every morning to give me a lesson of an hour and a half."

But the person of most moment at this time was undoubtedly the Contessina Emilia Viviani, whom, accompanied by Pacchiani, Claire, then Mary, and then Shelley, visited at the Convent of Sant' Anna. This beautiful girl, with profuse black hair, Grecian profile, and dreamy eyes, placed in the convent till she should be married, to satisfy the jealousy of her stepmother, became naturally an object of extreme interest to the Shelleys. Many visits were paid, and Mary invited her to stay with them at Christmas. Shelley was convinced that she had great talent, if not genius. Shelley and Mary sent her books, and Claire gave her English lessons at her convent, while she was taking a holiday from the Bojtis. Many letters are preserved from the beautiful Emilia to Shelley and Mary, letters which, translated into English, seem overflowing with sentiment and affection, but which to Italians would indicate rather the style cultivated by Italian ladies, which, to this day, seems one of their chief accomplishments if they are not gifted with a voice to sing. To Mary she complains of a certain coldness, but certainly this could not be brought to the charge of Shelley, who was now inspired to write his *Epipsychidion*. To him Emilia was as the Skylark, an emanation of the beautiful; but to Mary for a time, during Shelley's transitory adoration, the event evidently became painful, with all her philosophy and belief in her husband. She could not regard the lovely girl who took walks with him as the skylark that soared over their heads; and the *Epipsychidion* was evidently not a favourite poem of Mary.

Surely we may ascribe to this time, in the spring of 1821, the poem written by Shelley to Lieutenant Williams, whose acquaintance he had made in January. There is no month affixed to—

The Serpent is cast out from Paradise....

and it might well apply, with its reference to "my cold home," to the time when Mary, in depression and pique, did not always give her likewise sensitive husband all the welcome he was accustomed to, and Shelley took refuge in a poem by way of letter; for this is the time referred to by Mary in her letter to Claire as their seventh unfortunate spring—a mixture of Emilia and a Chancery suit! It was not till the next spring that Emilia was married, and led her husband and mother-in-law, as Mary puts it, "a devil of a life." *We* have only to be grateful to Emilia for having inspired one of the most wondrous poems in any language.

The Williamses, to whom Shelley's poem is addressed, were met by them in January. Mary writes of the fascinating Jane (Mrs. Williams) that she is certainly very pretty, but wants animation; while Shelley writes that she is extremely pretty and gentle, but apparently not very clever; that he liked her much, but had only seen her for an hour.

Mary, among her multifarious reading, notes an article by Medwin on Animal Magnetism, and Shelley, who suffered severely at this time, shortly afterwards tried its effect through Medwin. The latter bored Mary excessively; possibly she found the magnetising a wearisome operation, although Shelley is said to have been relieved by it. His highly nervous temperament was evidently impressed. When Medwin left, Mrs. Williams undertook to carry on the cure.

The Chancery suit referred to by Mary was an attempt between Sir Timothy's attorney and Shelley's to throw their affairs into Chancery, causing great alarm to them in Italy, till Horace Smith came to their rescue in England, and with indignant letters settled the inconsiderate litigation.

Mrs. Shelley, in her Notes to Poems in 1821, recounts how Shelley was nearly drowned, by a flat boat which he had recently acquired being overturned in the canal near Pisa, when returning from Leghorn. Williams upset the boat by standing up and holding the mast. Henry Reveley, Mrs. Gisborne's son, rescued Shelley and brought him to land, where he fainted with the cold. At this same time, at Pisa, Mary had to consider with Shelley a matter of great importance to Claire.

Byron, now at Ravenna, had placed Allegra, as already stated, in the convent of Bagnacavallo. He told Mrs. Hoppner that she had become so unmanageable by servants that it was necessary to have her under better care than he could secure, and he considered that it would be preferable to bring her up as a Roman Catholic with an Italian education, as in that way, with a fortune of five or six thousand pounds, she would marry an Italian and be provided for, whereas she would always hold an anomalous position in England. At this proposal Claire was extremely indignant; but Shelley and Mary took the opposite view, and considered that Byron acted for the best, as the convent was in a healthy position, and the nuns would be kind to the child. This idea of Mary would naturally be agreed with by some, and disapproved of by others; but at that time there was certainly no cause to indicate that Bagnacavallo would be more fatal to Allegra than any other place, although Claire's apprehensions were cruelly realised. From this time Claire and Byron wrote letters of recrimination to each other, which, considering Byron's obduracy against the feelings of the mother, Shelley and Mary came to hold as tyrannically unfeeling.

In May, Shelley and his wife and son returned to the baths of San Giuliano, and while here Shelley's *Adonais* was published. In 1820, when the Shelleys heard of Keats's fatal illness from Mrs. Gisborne, she having met him the day after he had received his death warrant from the doctor, they were the first to beg him to join them at Pisa. A small touch of poetical criticism, however, appears to have weighed more with the sensitive Keats than these friendly considerations for his health, and as he was about to accompany his friend Mr. Severn to Rome, he did not accept their kind offer, though in all probability Pisa would have been better for him.

During this summer at the baths Mary had finished her romance of *Valperga*, and read it to her husband, who admired it extremely. He considered it to be a "living and moving picture of an age almost forgotten, a profound study of the passions of human nature."

Valperga, published in 1823, the year after Shelley's death, is a romance of the 14th century in Italy, during the height of the struggle between the Guelphs and the Ghibellines, when each state and almost each town was at war with the other; a condition of things which lends itself to romance. Mary Shelley's intimate acquaintance with Italy and Italians gives her the necessary knowledge to write on this subject. Her zealous Italian studies came to her aid, and her love of nature give life and vitality to the scene. Valperga, the ancestral castle home of Euthanasia, a Florentine lady of the Guelph faction, is most picturesquely described, on its ledge of projecting rock, overlooking the plain of Lucca; the dependent peasants around happy under the protection of their good Signora. That this beautiful and high-minded lady should be affianced to a Ghibelline leader is a natural combination; but when her lover Castruccio, prince of Lucca, carries his political enthusiasm the length of making war on her native city of Florence, whose Republican greatness and love of art are happily described, Euthanasia cannot let love stand in the way of duty and gratitude to all those dearest to her. The severe struggle is well described, for Euthanasia has loved Castruccio from their childhood. When they played about the mountain grounds of her home at Valperga, Castruccio learnt the secret paths to the Castle, which knowledge later helped him to take the fortress when Euthanasia refused to yield it to him. Castruccio's character is also well described: his devoted attachment to Euthanasia from which nothing could turn him, till the passions of the conqueror and party faction are still stronger; and the irresistible force which impels him to make war and subdue the Guelphs, which by her is regarded as murder and rapine, disunites beings seemingly formed for each other. All these different emotions are portrayed with great beauty and simplicity.

The Italian superstitions are well shown, as how the Florentines ascribed all good and evil fortune to conjunction of stars. The power of the Inquisition in Rome comes likewise into play, when the beautiful prophetess Beatrice (the child of the prophetess Wilhelmina) who had to be given to the Leper for protection, as even his filthy and deserted hut was safer for her than that it should be known to the Inquisition that she existed. She is rescued from the Leper by a bishop who heard her story from the deathbed of the woman to whom her mother when dying had confided her. She was then brought up by the bishop's sister. Her mother's spirit of prophecy was inherited by the daughter; and as the mother believed herself to be an emanation of the Holy Spirit, so Beatrice thought herself the Ancilla Dei. These mystical fancies and their working are depicted with much beauty and strength.

These Donne Estatiche first appear in Italy after the 12th century, and had continued to the time which Mary Shelley selected for her romance. After giving an account of their pretensions, Muratori gravely observes: "We may piously believe that some were distinguished by supernatural gifts and admitted to the secrets of heaven, but we may justly suspect that the source of many of their revelations was their ardent imagination filled with ideas of religion and piety." Beatrice, on prophesying the Ghibelline rule in Ferrara, is seized by the emissaries of the Pope, and has to undergo the ordeal of the white hot ploughshares, through which she passes unscathed, there having apparently been connivance to help her through. Her exultation and enthusiasm become intense, and it is only after a great shock that she grows conscious of the falseness of her position; for, having met Castruccio on his mission to Ferrara, she is irresistibly attracted by him, and, mixing up her infatuation with her mystical ideas, does not hesitate to make secret appointments with him, never doubting that her love is returned, and that they are one at heart. When at length Castruccio has to return to Lucca, and to his betrothed, Euthanasia, the shock to the poor mystical Beatrice is terrible. Finally she is met as a pilgrim wending her weary way to Rome. Assuredly, Shelley was justified in admiring this character. There is a straightforwardness in the plot into which the stormy history of the period is clearly introduced, which gives much interest to this romance, and it is a decided advance upon *Frankenstein*, though her age when that was written must not be forgotten. A book of this kind shows forcibly the troubles to which a lovely country like Italy is exposed through disunion, and must fill the hearts of all lovers of this beautiful land with gratitude to the noble men who willingly sacrificed themselves to help in the cause of united Italy; those whose songs roused the people, and carried hope into the hearts of even the prisoners in the pozzi of Venice; for the man of idea who can rouse the nation by his songs does not help less than the brave soldier who can aid with his arms, though alas! he does not always live to see the triumph he has helped to achieve. [Footnote: Gabriele Rossetti, whom Mary Shelley knew, and to whom she referred for information while writing her lives of Italian poets, has been said to have been the first who in modern times had the idea of a united Italy under a constitutional monarch, for which idea and for his rousing songs he was forced to leave Italy by Ferdinand I. of Naples in 1821, and remained an exile in England till his death in 1854, at the age of 71. How Mary Shelley, with her husband, must have sympathised in these ideas with their love of Italy can be understood, although it was the climate and beauty of Italy more than the people that charmed Shelley; but then was he not also an exile from his native land?]

This work, when completed, was sent to her father by Mary, for it had been a labour of love, and the sum of four hundred pounds which Godwin obtained for it was devoted to help him in his difficulties. Unhappily, the romance was not published till the year after her husband's death.

CHAPTER XII.

LAST MONTHS WITH SHELLEY.

IN July 1821, Shelley left his wife at the baths while he went to seek a house at Florence for the winter; but he returned in three days unsuccessful. He then received a letter from Byron begging him to go straight to Ravenna, various matters having to be talked over. Shelley left at two in the afternoon, on his birthday, August 4th. Here he had to go through the Paolo-Hoppner scandal, which we have referred to. Shelley had to write letters to Mary on the subject, and Mary wrote the most indignant and decisive denial of the imputation, on her husband and Claire. She writes: "I swear by the life of my child, by my blessed beloved child, that I know the accusations to be false." If more were needed, the clear exposition by Mr. Jeaffreson and later Professor Dowden, leave nothing to be said. Shelley wrote to Mary describing his visit to Allegra at the convent, where he found her prettily dressed in white muslin with an apron of black silk. She was a most graceful, airy child; she took Shelley all over the convent, and began ringing the nun's call-bell, without being reprimanded—although the prioress had considerable trouble to prevent the nuns assembling dressed or undressed—which struck Shelley as showing that she was kindly treated. Before leaving Ravenna, about August 17th, he wrote to thank his wife for her promise of her miniature, done by Williams, which he received a few days later from her at the Baths of Pisa. Mary and Shelley both were of those who, wherever they found a friend, found also a pensioner, or person to be benefited by them; as they did not seek their friends for personal advantage, and were among those who hold it more blessed to give than to receive. In January 1821, Mrs. Leigh Hunt wrote to Mary Shelley, begging her to help her husband and family to come to Italy—he was ill and depressed, and surrounded by all his children sick and suffering. While Shelley was at Ravenna he brought up this subject with Byron, who proposed that he, Shelley, and Leigh Hunt should start a periodical for their joint works, and share the profits. Shelley did not agree to this for himself, as he was not popular, and could only gain advantage from the others; but for Hunt it was different, and Shelley joyfully wrote to him from Pisa, on his return from Ravenna, to join them as soon as possible. Delays occurred in Hunt's departure, and Byron received letters from England warning him against joining with Shelley and Hunt. Byron arrived in Pisa with the Countess Guiccioli and her brother Pietro Gamba, on November the 1st, at the Lanfranchi Palace, and the Shelleys had apartments at the top of I Tre Palazzi di Chiesa, opposite. Claire, who had been staying with them, and accompanied them on a trip to Spezzia, had now returned to Professor Bojti's at Florence.

Mary had the task of furnishing the ground floor of Byron's Lanfranchi Palace for the Hunts, although Byron insisted on paying for it. Hunt, meanwhile, was unable to proceed beyond Plymouth that winter, where they were obliged to stay by stress of weather and Mrs. Hunt's illness. Thus some months passed by, during which time Byron lost the first ardour of the enterprise, and became very lukewarm. It must have been when Mary had good reason to foresee this result that she wrote to Hunt thus:—

MY DEAR FRIEND,

I know that S. has some idea of persuading you to come here. I am too ill to write the reasonings, only let me entreat you let no persuasions induce you to come; selfish feelings you may be sure do not dictate me, but it would be complete madness to come. I wish I could write more. I wish I were with you to assist you. I wish I could break my chains and leave this dungeon. Adieu, I shall hear about yon and Marianne's health from S.

Ever your M.

Shelley was forced to apply to Byron to help him with money to lend Hunt, and Byron had ceased to care about the *Liberal*, the projected magazine.

While staying near Byron the Shelleys came in for a large influx of visitors, often much to Shelley's annoyance, and Mary wrote of their wish, if Greece were liberated, of settling in one of the lovely islands.

The middle of January brought one visitor to the Shelleys, who, introduced by the Williams, became more than a passing figure in Mary's life. In Edward John Trelawny she found a staunch friend ever after. Trelawny, who had led a wild life from the time he left the navy in mere boyhood, was a conspicuous character wherever known. With small reverence for the orthodox creeds, he must have had some of the traits of the ancient Vikings, before meeting Shelley; but from that time he became his devoted admirer, or, as one has observed who knew him, as Ahab at Elijah's feet, so Trelawny at Shelley's was ready to humble himself for the first time; nor did he afterwards, to the end of a long life, ever speak of him without veneration. Shelley's exalted ideas touched a chord in the strong man's heart, and within a few weeks of his death he rejoiced in hearing of a crowded assembly in Glasgow, enthusiastic in hearing a lecture on Shelley, and asserted it is the "spirit of poetry which needs spreading now; science is popular to the exclusion of poetry as a regenerator."

The day after their first meeting with Trelawny, Mary notes in her diary how Trelawny discussed with Williams and Shelley about building a boat which they desired to have, and which Captain Roberts was to build at Genoa without delay. A year later Mary added a note to this entry, to the effect how she and Jane Williams then laughed at the way their husbands decided without consulting them, though they agreed in hating the boat. She adds: "How well I remember that night! How short-sighted we are! And now that its anniversary is come and gone, methinks I cannot be the wretch I too truly am." This winter, at Pisa, Mary, with popular and strong men to protect her, was not neglected so much as hitherto. She went to Mrs. Beauclerc's ball with Trelawny; but she refers to a strange feeling of depression in the midst of a gay assembly.

On February 8 Shelley started, with Williams, to seek for houses in the neighbourhood of Spezzia; the idea being that the Shelleys, the Williamses, Trelawny and Captain Roberts, Byron, Countess Guiccioli and her brother, should all spend the summer there, although Mary feared the party would be too large for unity. Only one suitable house could be found; but Shelley was not to be stopped by such a trifle, and the house must do for all.

In the early spring of this year, Mary wrote to Mrs. Hunt how she and Mrs. Williams went violet-hunting, while the men went on longer expeditions. The Shelleys and their surroundings must have kept the English assembled in Pisa in a pleasing state of excitement. At one time Mary caused a commotion by attending Dr. Nott's Sunday service, which was held on the ground floor of her house. On one occasion he preached against Atheism, and, having specially asked Mary to attend, it was taken as a marked attack on Shelley, and it was considered that Mary had taken part against her husband.

Mary wrote a pathetic letter to Mrs. Gisborne that she had only been three times to church, and now longed to be in some sea-girt isle with Shelley and her baby, but that Shelley was entangled with Byron and could not get away. She was longing for the time by the sea when she would have boats and horses.

While Mary was yearning for sympathy with her kind, or solitude with Shelley, he for a time was wasting regrets that she did not sympathise with or feel his poetry. It was the old story of the Skylark. While he was seeking inspiration at some fresh source, Mary did not become equally enthusiastic about the new idea. But most probably, in spite of Trelawny's later notion and her own self-reproaches of not having done all possible things to sympathise with Shelley, Mary's behaviour was really the best calculated for his comfort. A man who did not like regular meals and conventional habits in this respect, would not have liked his wife to worry him constantly on the subject, and the plate of cold meat and bread placed on a shelf, as his table was probably covered with papers—which Trelawny found there forgotten, towards the end of a "lost day" as Shelley called it—was not inappropriate for one who forgot his meals and did not like being teased. Mary was not of the nature to make, nor Shelley of the nature to require, a docile slave; and during the time at Naples, for which Mary felt most regret, Shelley wrote of her as "a dear friend with whom added years old intercourse adds to my appreciation of its value, and who would have more right than anyone to complain that she has not been able to extinguish in me the very power of delineating sadness."

During this time the English visitors believed and manufactured all kinds of stories about the eccentric English then at Pisa. Trelawny had been murdered—Byron wounded—and Taaffe was guarded by bulldogs in Byron's house! These rumours were laughed over by the people concerned.

On one occasion Mrs. Shelley, with the Countess Guiccioli, witnessed from their carriage the affair with the dragoon Masi, when he jostled against Taaffe. Byron, Shelley, and Gamba pursued him; Shelley, coming up with him first, was knocked down, but was rescued by Captain Hay. The dragoon was finally wounded by one of Byron's servants, under the idea that he had wounded Byron.

During this exciting time at Pisa, Claire was eating her heart at Florence with longings and regrets for Allegra; and Mary and Shelley were trying to calm her by letters, and growing themselves more and more dissatisfied at Byron's treatment of the mother. There are entries in Claire's diary as to her cough, and the last entry before the day she left Florence for Pisa—April 13—is erased. Then there is one of her ominous blanks from April till September.

While Claire travelled with Williams and his wife to Spezzia to look for a house, news came from Bagnacavallo which verified her worst fears. Typhus fever had ravaged the convent and district, and the fragile blossom had succumbed. Shelley and Mary determined to keep this "evil news," as Mary calls it, from Claire till she is away from the neighbourhood of Byron. So, on her return from the unsuccessful visit to Spezzia, they have to conceal their sorrow and their feelings. Shelley, ever anxious for Claire's distress, persuaded her to accompany Mary to Spezzia, saying they must take any house they could get. Claire had thought of returning to Florence, but was overruled by Shelley, who, as Mary wrote to Mrs. Gisborne, carried all like a torrent before him and sent Mary and Claire with Trelawny to Spezzia. Shelley followed with their furniture in boats; and so, on April 26, they were hurried by Shelley, or fate, from misfortune to misfortune, in taking Claire to a haven where she might be helped to bear her sore trouble. Mary, with her companions, secured the only available house—Casa Magui, at San Terenzio, near Lerici—in which it was settled that they and the Williamses must find room and bring their furniture. Difficulties of all kinds had to be overcome from the dogana. The furniture arrived in boats, and they were told the dues upon it would amount to three hundred pounds, but the harbour-master kindly allowed it to be removed to the villa as to a depôt till further orders arrived. Then there were the difficulties of Mrs. Williams, of whom Shelley wrote that she was pining for her saucepans. Claire felt the necessity of returning to Florence, the space being so small. This, however, was not to be thought of. Claire still had to have the news of her child's death broken to her, and Mrs. Williams's room had to be used for secret consultations. Claire, entering the room and seeing the agitated silence on her approach, at once realised the state of the case. She felt her Allegra was dead, and it only devolved on Shelley to tell the sad tale of a fever-ravaged district, and a fever-tossed child dying among the kind nuns, who are ever good nurses. Claire's grief was intense; but all that she now wanted was a sight of her child's coffin, a likeness of her, and a lock of her golden hair (a portion of which last is now in the writer's possession). The latter Shelley helped to obtain for her; but Claire never after forgave him who had consigned her child to the convent in the Romagna, nor allowed her another sight of her little one.

On May 21 Claire left for Florence, and Mary remained with her husband and the Williamses at Casa Magni. These rapidly succeeding troubles, together with Mary's being again in a delicate state of health, left the circle in an unhinged and nervous state of apprehension. Shelley saw visions of Allegra rising from the sea, clapping her hands and smiling at him. Mrs. Williams saw Shelley on the balcony, and then he was nowhere near, nor had he been there. Shelley ranged from wild delight with the beauty around him, to such fits of despondency as when he most culpably proposed to Mrs. Williams, while in a boat with him and her babies, in the bay—"Now let us together solve the great mystery." But she managed to get him to turn shorewards, and escaped at the first opportunity from the boat.

Mary was not without her prophetic periods—a deep melancholy settled on her amid the lovely scenery. Generally at home with mountain and water, she now only felt oppressed by their proximity. Shelley was at work on the *Triumph of Life*, one of his grandest poems; but Mary was always apprehensive except when with her husband, least so when lying in a boat with her head on his knees. If Shelley were absent, she feared for Percy, her son, so that, in spite of the oasis of peace and rest and beauty around them, she was weak and nervous; and Shelley, for fear of hurting her, had to conceal such matters as might trouble her, especially the again critical state of the affairs of her father, who was in want of four hundred pounds to compound with his creditors. These alarms for Mary's health and tranquillity of mind, and the consequent necessity of keeping any trying subject from her, may have induced Shelley in writing to Claire to adopt a confidential tone not otherwise advisable.

While at Casa Magni, the fatal boat which had been discussed on the first evening Trelawny spent with the Shelleys, arrived. The "perfect plaything for the summer" had been built against the advice of Trelawny, by a Genoese ship-builder, after a model obtained by Lieutenant Williams from one of the royal dockyards in England. Originally it was intended to call it the *Don Juan*, but recent circumstances had caused a break in the intimacy of Shelley with Byron, and Shelley felt that this would be eternal. He, therefore, no longer wished any name to remind him of Byron, and gave the name *Ariel*, proposed by Trelawny, to the small craft. With considerable difficulty the name *Don Juan* was taken from the sail, where Byron had manoeuvred to have it painted.

Towards the end of May, Mary was seriously suffering; the difficulties of housekeeping for the Williamses as well as themselves were no trifle. Provisions had to be fetched from a distance of over three miles. Shelley writes to Claire, hoping she will be able to find them a man-cook. As Mary was somewhat better when Shelley wrote, he feared he should have to speak to her about Godwin's affairs, but put off the evil day.

On June 6 we find Shelley setting out with Williams in the *Ariel* to meet Claire on her way from Florence to Casa Magni. A calm having delayed them till the evening, they were too late to meet Claire, who travelled on by land for Via Reggio. Shelley and Williams, returning by sea, arrived home a short time before her. Their return and her arrival were none too soon; for, on the 8th or 9th, Mary fell dangerously ill, as she wrote in August to Mrs. Gisborne: "I was so ill that for seven hours I lay nearly lifeless—kept from fainting by brandy, vinegar, eau-de-cologne, &c. At length ice was brought to our solitude; it came before the doctor, so Claire and Jane were afraid of using it; but Shelley over-ruled them, and, by an unsparing application of it, I was restored. They all thought, and so did I at one time, that I was about to die."

Shelley, equal to the occasion, felt the strain on his nerves afterwards, and a week after his wife was out of danger he alarmed her greatly, as she relates: "While yet unable to walk, I was confined to my bed. In the middle of the night I was awoke by hearing him scream, and come rushing into my room; I was sure that he was asleep, and tried to waken him by calling on him; but he continued to scream, which inspired me with such a panic that I jumped out of bed and ran across the hall to Mrs. Williams's room, where I fell through weakness, though I was so frightened that I got up again immediately. She let me in, and Williams went to Shelley who had been wakened by my getting out of bed. He said that he had not been asleep, and that it was a vision that he saw that had frightened him. But as he declared that he had not screamed, it was certainly a dream, and no waking vision." And so the lovely summer months passed by with all these varying emotions, with thoughts soaring to the highest pinnacles of imagination as in the *Triumph of Life*, and with the enjoyment of the high ideals of others, as in reading the Spanish dramas: music also gave enchantment when Jane Williams played her guitar. With the intense beauty of the scenery, and the wildness of the natives who used sometimes to dance all night on the sands in front of their house; the emotions of life seemed compressed into this time, spent in what would be considered by many great dulness, in the company of Trelawny and the Williamses. And now an event, long hoped for, arrived, for the Hunts were in the harbour of Genoa, and Shelley was to meet them at Leghorn, as Hunt's letter, which reached them on June 19, had been delayed too long to allow of Shelley joining them at Genoa. On July I intelligence came of the Hunts' departure from Genoa; and at noon a breeze rising from the west decided the desirability of at once starting for Leghorn. Shelley, with Captain Roberts who had joined him at Lerici, arrived by nine in the evening, after the officers of health had left their office. The voyagers were thus unable to land that evening, but spent the time alongside of Byron's yacht, the *Bolivar*, from which they received coverings for the night.

The next morning news arrived from Byron's villa, which already began to verify Mary's forebodings in her letter to Hunt, and proved the clear-sightedness of her forecast. Disturbances having taken place at his house at Monte Nero, Count Gamba and his family were banished by the Government from Tuscany, and there were rumours that Byron might be leaving immediately for America or Switzerland. This was indeed trying news for Shelley to have to break to the Hunts on their first meeting in the hotel at Leghorn, where, after four years, the two friends again met. The encounter was most touching, as remembered years later by Thornton Hunt. Shelley had plenty of work on hand for a few days; he procured Vacca, the physician, for Mrs. Hunt; and had to sustain his friend during his anxiety as to his wife's health and the uncertainty as to Byron's conduct. Shelley would not think of leaving him till he had seen him comfortably installed in the Lanfranchi Palace, in the rooms which Mary had prepared for him at Byron's request. The still more difficult task of fixing Byron to some promise of assistance with regard to the *Liberal* was likewise carried out; and after one or two days of dejection, during which Shelley wrote to Mrs. Williams on July 4 to relieve his own despondency, and to his wife to relieve hers, as her depression of spirits required more cheering than adding to, he wrote:—"How are you, my best Mary? Write especially how is your health and how your spirits are, and whether you are not more reconciled to staying at Lerici, at least during the summer. You have no idea how I am hurried and occupied. I have not a moment's leisure, but will write by the next post."

Soon after writing these letters, Shelley found with exultation that his work was done. As usual, he had carried all before him, and secured Byron's "Vision of Judgment" for the first number of the *Liberal*, and by July 7 he was able to show his friends the ever-delightful sights of Pisa. Thus one day of rest and pleasure remained to Shelley after doing his utmost to assist his friend Hunt. To the last Shelley was faithful to his aim—that of doing all he could for others. His interviews with Byron had secured a return of the friendly feeling which nought but death was henceforth to sever, and the two great names, which nothing can divide, are linked by the unbreakable chain of genius—genius, the fire of the universe, which at times may flicker low, but which, bursting into flame here and there, illumines the dark recesses of the soul of the universe—genius which has made the world we know, which, never absent, though dormant, has changed the stone to the flower, the flower to animal, and, gaining ever in degree through the various stages of life, is the divine attribute, the will, the idea. Genius manifest in the greatest and best of humanity, shown indeed, as the Word of God, or as he who holds the mirror up to nature, or by the great power which in colour or monotone can display the love and agony of a dying Christ; by the loving poet, who can soar beyond his age to uphold an unselfish aim of perfection to the world; by all those who, throwing off their mortal attributes at times, can live the true life free from the too absorbing pleasures of the flesh, which can only he enjoyed by dividing.

But now Shelley's mortal battle was nearly over; he who had not let his talent or myriad talents lie dormant was to rest, his work of life was nearly done. Not that the good is ever ended; verily, through thousands of generations, through eternity, it endures; while the bad—perhaps not useless—is the chaff which is dispersed, and which has no result unless to hurry on the divine will. Our life is double. Shelley's atoms were to return to their primal elements. The unknown atoms or attributes of them were undoubtedly to carry on their work; he had added to the eternal intellect.

The last facts of Shelley's life are related by Trelawny and by Mrs. Shelley. On the morning of July 8, having finished his arrangements for the Hunts and spent one day in showing the noble sights of Pisa, Shelley, after making purchases for their house and obtaining money from his banker, accompanied by Trelawny during the forenoon, was ready by noon to embark on the *Ariel* with Edward Williams and the sailor-boy, Charles Vivian. Captain Roberts was not without apprehensions as to the weather, and urged Shelley to delay his departure for a day; but Williams was anxious to rejoin his wife, and Shelley not in a humour to frustrate his wishes. Trelawny, who desired to accompany them in the *Bolivar* into the offing, was prevented, not having obtained his health order, and so could only reluctantly remain behind and watch his friends' small craft through a ship's glass.

Mistakes were noted, the ship's mate of the *Bolivar* remarking they ought to have started at daybreak instead of after one o'clock; that they were too near shore; that there would soon be a land breeze; the gaff top-sail was foolish in a boat with no deck and no sailor on board; and then, pointing to the southwest, "Look at those black lines and dirty rags hanging on them out of the sky; look at the smoke on the water; the devil is brewing mischief."

The approaching storm was watched also by Captain Roberts from the light-house, whence he saw the topsail taken in; then the vessel freighted with such precious life was seen no more in the mist of the storm. For a time the sea seemed solidified and appeared as of lead, with an oily scum; the wind did not ruffle it. Then sounds of thunder, wind, and rain filled the air; these lasted with fury for twenty minutes; then a lull, and anxious looks among the boats which had rushed into the harbour for Shelley's bark. No glass could find it on the horizon. Trelawny landed at eight o'clock; inquiries were useless. An oar was seen on a fishing boat: it might be English—it might be Shelley's; but this was denied. Nothing to do but wait, till the third day, when he returned to Pisa to tell his fears to Hunt and Byron, who could only listen with quivering lips and speak with faltering voice.

While these friends were agitated between hope and fear, the time was passing wearily at San Terenzio. Jane Williams received a letter from her husband on that day (written on Saturday from Leghorn), where he was waiting for Shelley. It stated that if they did not return on Monday, he certainly would be back at the latest on Thursday in a felucca by himself if necessary. The fatal Monday passed amid storm and rain, and no idea was entertained by Mrs. Shelley or Mrs. Williams that their husbands had started in such weather as they experienced. Mary, who had then scarcely recovered from her dangerous illness, and was unable to join Claire and Jane Williams in their evening walks, could only pace up and down in the verandah and feel oppressed by the very beauty which surrounded her. So till Wednesday these days of storm and oppression and undefined fears passed; then, some feluccas arriving from Leghorn, they were informed that their husbands had left on Monday; but that could not be believed. Thursday came and passed, *the* Thursday which should be the latest for Williams's arrival. The wind had been fair, but midnight arrived, and still Mary and Jane were alone; then sad hope gave place to fearful anxiety preceding despair; but Friday was letter day—wait for that—and no boat could leave. Noon of Friday and letters came, but *to*, not *from* Shelley. Hunt wrote to him: "Pray write to tell us how you got home, for they say that you had bad weather after you sailed on Monday, and we are anxious." Mary read so far when the paper fell from her hands and she trembled all over. Jane read it, and said, "It is all over." Mary replied, "No, my dear Jane, it is not all over; but this suspense is dreadful. Come with me; we will go to *Leghorn*; we will post, to be swift and learn our fate."

Thus, as Mary Shelley herself describes, they crossed to Lerici, despair in their hearts, two poor, wild, aghast creatures driving, "like Matilda," towards the sea to know if they were to be for ever doomed to misery. The idea of seeing Hunt for the first time after four years, to ask "Where is he?" nearly drove Mary into convulsions. On knocking at the door of the Casa Lanfranchi they found Lord Byron was in Pisa and. Hunt being in bed, their interview was to be with Byron, only to hear, "They knew nothing. He had left Pisa on Sunday; on Monday he had sailed. There had been bad weather Monday afternoon; more they knew not." Mary, who had risen from, a bed of sickness for the journey, and had travelled all day, had now at midnight to proceed to Leghorn in search of Trelawny; for what rest could there be with such a terrible doubt hanging over their lives? They could not despair, for that would have been death; they had to pass through longer hours and days of anguish to subdue their souls to bear the inevitable.

They reached Leghorn, and were driven to the wrong inn. Nothing to do but wait till the morning—but wait dressed till six o'clock—when they proceeded to other inns and found Captain Roberts. His face showed that the worst was true. They only heard how their husbands had set out. Still hope was not dead; might not their husbands be at Corsica or Elba? It was said they had been seen in the Gulf. They resolved to return; but now not alone, for Trelawny accompanied them. Agony succeeded agony; the water they crossed told Mary it was his grave.

While crossing the bay they saw San Terenzio illuminated for a festa, while despair was in their hearts. The days passed, a week ever counted as two by Mary, and then, when she was very ill, Trelawny, who had been long expected from his search, returned, and now they knew that all was over, for the bodies had been cast on shore. One was a tall, slight figure, with Sophocles in one pocket of the jacket, and Keats's last poems in the other; the poetry he loved remained; his body a mere mutilated corpse, which for a while had enshrined such divine intellect. Williams's corpse, also, was found some miles distant, still more unrecognisable, save for the black silk handkerchief tied sailor-fashion round his neck; and after some ten days a third body was found, a mere skeleton., supposed to be the sailor-boy, Charles Vivian.

"Is there no hope?" Mary asked, when Trelawny reappeared on July 19. He could not answer, but left the room, and sent the servant to take the children to their widowed mothers. He then, on the 20th, took them from the sound of the cruel waves to the Hunts at Pisa.

Naught remained now but to perform the last funeral rites. Mary decided that Shelley should rest with his dearly-loved son in the English cemetery in Rome. With some little difficulty, Trelawny obtained permission, with the kind assistance of the English Chargé d'Affaires at Florence, Mr. Dawkins, to have the bodies burned on the shore, according to the custom of bodies cast up from the sea, so that the ashes could be removed without fear of infection. The iron furnace was made at Leghorn, of the dimensions of a human body, according to Trelawny's orders; and on August 15 the body of Lieutenant Williams was disinterred from the sand where it had been buried when cast up. Byron recognised him by his clothes and his teeth. The funeral rites were performed by Trelawny by throwing incense, salt, and wine on the pyre, according to classic custom; and when nothing remained but some black ashes and small pieces of white bone, these were placed by Trelawny in one of the oaken boxes he had provided for the purpose, and then consigned to Byron and Hunt. The next day another pyre was raised, and again the soldiers had to dig for the body, buried in lime. When placed in the furnace it was three hours before the consuming body showed the still unconsumed heart, which Trelawny saved from the furnace, snatching it out with his hand; and there, amidst the Italian beauty, on the Italian shore, was consumed the body of the poet who held out immortal hope to his kind, who, in advance of the scientists, held it as a noble fact that humanity was progressive; who, more for this than for his unfortunate first marriage and its unhappy sequel, was banished by his countrymen, and held as nothing by his generation. But, as Claire wrote later in her diary, "It might be said of him, as Cicero said of Rome, 'Ungrateful England shall not possess my bones.'"

The ashes of the body were placed in the oaken box; those of the heart, handed by Trelawny to Hunt, were afterwards given into the possession of Mary, who jealously guarded them during her life, in a place where they were found at her death, in a silken case, in which was kept a Pisan copy of the *Adonais*. The ashes of Shelley's body were finally buried in the cemetery in Rome, where the grave of the English poet is now one of the strongest links between the present and the past world; and there beside him rest now the ashes of his faithful friend, Trelawny, who survived him nearly sixty years.

CHAPTER XIII.

WIDOWHOOD.

The last ceremony was over, hope, fear, despair, were past, and Mary Shelley had to recommence her life, or death in life, her one solace her little son, her one resource for many years her work. Fortunately for her, her education and her studious habits were a shield against the cold world which she had to encounter, and her accustomed personal economy, which had fitted her to be the worthy companion to her generous husband, whom she had encouraged rather than thwarted in his constantly recurring acts of philanthropy, would help her in her present struggle; and one friend was ready to assist with advice and out of his then slender means, Mr. Trelawny. But from England no help was forthcoming. Godwin's affairs having reached the climax of bankruptcy already referred to, were not likely to settle down easily now that the ever-ready supply was suddenly cut short.

Sir Timothy Shelley was not inclined to continue the terms he made with his son, nor was anything to be arranged but on conditions which Mrs. Shelley could never consent to. Of her despondent state of misery we can judge in her letters of 1822 to Claire, as when she writes from Genoa, September 15, "This hateful Genoa"; and, describing her misery on her husband's death, she exclaims: "Well, I shall have his books and his MSS., and in these I shall live, and from the study of these I do expect some instants of content.... some seconds of exaltation that may render me both happier here, and more worthy of him hereafter." Then, "There is nothing but unhappiness to me, if indeed I except Trelawny, who appears so truly generous and kind.... Nothing but the horror of being a burden to my family prevents my accompanying Jane (to England). If I had any fixed income, I should go at least to Paris, and I shall go the moment I have one." And again in December of the same year she writes to Claire, addressing her as Mdlle. de Clairmont, *chez* Mdme. de Hennistein, Vienna. She mentions an approach to Sir Timothy, through lawyers, abortive as yet; how she detests Genoa; "Hunt does not like me." Her daily routine is copying Shelley's manuscripts and reading Greek; in her despair, study is her only relief. She sees no one but Lord Byron, and the Guiccioli once a mouth, Trelawny seldom, and he is on the eve of his departure for Leghorn.

Thus we find Mary Shelley going on from day to day, too poor to travel so far as Paris, as yet her child and her work of love on her husband's MS. filling up her time, till in February she had to undergo the mortification of her father-in-law proposing that she should give her son up entirely to him, and in return receive a settled income. But Mary was not of those who can be either bought or sold, and, having the means of subsistence in herself, she could be independent; a letter from her father shows how they were at one on this important subject, and it must have been a great encouragement to her in her loneliness, as she was always diffident of her own powers. However, now her work lay in arranging and copying her husband's MSS., and saving treasures which but for her loving care might have been lost. In the spring of this year, 1823, Trelawny was in Rome arranging Shelley's grave, which he bought with the adjoining ground for himself, and he had the massive slab of stone placed there which still tells of the "*Cor cordium*" In the autumn of the same year Mary found means for leaving the hated Genoa, and, travelling through France; she stayed for a time at Versailles with her father's old friends, the Kennys, and of this visit one of the daughters, now Mrs. Cox, then a child of about six years, retains a lively and pleasing recollection. Brought up in France and imbued with the idea and pictures of the Madonna and child, the little girl, on seeing Mrs. Shelley arrive with her small son, became impressed with the idea that the pale, sweet, oval-laced lady was the Madonna come to visit them; and this idea was not dispelled by the gentle manner and kind way that she had with the children, reminding one who had been punished by mistake that the next time she was naughty she would have had her punishment in advance. This visit was followed later by the intimacy and friendship of the two families. In London (as we learn from a letter to Miss Holcroft, Mrs. Kenny's daughter, by her previous marriage with Holcroft) Mrs. Shelley was settled at 14, Sheldhurst Street, Brunswick Square. She was then hoping that her father-in-law would make her an allowance sufficient for her to live comfortably in dear Italy; and, at all events, she had received "a present supply, so that much good at least has been accomplished by my journey." She felt quite lost in London, and Percy had not yet learnt English. She had seen Lamb, but he did not remark on her being altered. She would then have returned to Italy, but her father did not like the idea.

Among other work at this time Mary Shelley attempted a drama, but in this her father did not encourage her, as he writes to her in February 1824 that her personages are mere abstractions, not men and women. Godwin does not regret that she has not dramatic talent, as the want of it will save her much trouble and mortification.

This disappointment did not discourage Mary, for in the next year she published, with Henry Colburn of New Burlington Street, her novel *The Last Man*, of which a second edition appeared in the succeeding year. This must have been a great help to Mary's limited means: she had received four hundred pounds for her previous romance.

During this year we find Mrs. Shelley living in Kentish Town, as she writes from that address to Trelawny in July 1824. She is much cheered by finding her old friend still remembers her. She speaks of him as her warm-hearted friend, the remnant of the happy days of her vagabond life in beloved Italy, and now, shortly before writing, she had seen another link in her past life disappear; for the hearse containing the body of Lord Byron had passed her window going up Highgate Hill, on his last journey to the seat of his ancestors. Mary had been much interested in the account Trelawny had sent her of Byron's latest moments. She had been to see the poet's remains at the house where they lay in London. She saw his valet, Fletcher, and "from a few words he imprudently let fall, it would seem that his Lordship spoke of C———— in his last moments, and of his wish to do something for her, at a time when his mind, vacillating between consciousness and delirium, would not permit him to do anything." She describes how Fletcher found Lady Byron in great grief, but inexorable, and how Byron's memoirs had been destroyed by Mrs. Leigh and Hobhouse, but adds: "There was not much in them, I know, for I read them some years ago at Venice; but the world fancied that it was to have a confession of the hidden feelings of one concerning whom they were always passionately curious." She says that Moore was much disgusted. He was writing a life of Byron, but it was considered that although he had had the MSS. so long in his hands, he had not found time to read them. She asks Trelawny to help Moore with any facts or details. Mary thanks Trelawny for his wish that she and Jane Williams, who see each other and little else every day, should join him in Greece. That is impossible, but she looks for him to come in the winter to England. She speaks of July as fatal to her for good and ill. "On this very very day"—she is writing July 28—"I went to France with my Shelley. How young, heedless, and happy and poor we were then, and now my sleeping boy is all that is left to me of that time— my boy and a thousand recollections which never sleep." She describes the pretty country lanes round Kentish Town. If only there were cloudless skies and orange sunsets, she would not mind the scenery; but she can attach herself to no one. She and Jane live alone; her child is in excellent health, a tall, fine, handsome boy. She is still in hopes that she will get an income of three or four hundred a year from Sir Timothy in a few months; one of her chief wishes in being independent would be to help Claire, who is in Russia. Of this time Claire wrote a good account in her diary.

These letters to Trelawny give much insight into the present life of Mary Shelley, and refer to much of interest in her past. On February 25 she tells how she had been with Jane, her father, and Count Gamba to see Kean in Othello, but she adds: "Yet, my dear friend, I wish we had seen it represented as was talked of at Pisa. Iago would never have found a better representative than that strange and wondrous creature whom one regrets daily more; for who can equal him?" Trelawny adds a note that in 1822 Byron had contemplated that he, Trelawny, Williams, Medwin, Mary Shelley, and Mrs. Williams were to take the several parts:—Byron, Iago; Trelawny, Othello; Mary, Desdemona. Trelawny adds that Byron recited a great portion of his part with great gusto, and looked it too. Byron said that all Pisa were to be the audience. Letters from Trelawny from Zante in 1826, carry on the correspondence. He regrets that poverty keeps them apart; speaks of the difficulty of travelling without money; he rejoices that he still holds a place in her affections, and says, "You know, Mary, that I always loved you impetuously and sincerely." In 1827, still writing from Kentish Town, on Easter Sunday, but saying that in future her address will be at her father's, 44, Gower Place, Bedford Square, we have another of her charming letters to her friend, full of good reflections. In this letter she tells how Jane Williams has united her life with that of Shelley's early friend, Mr. Jefferson Hogg. He had loved her devotedly since her arrival in England five years earlier, but till now she had been too constant to Williams's memory to accept him. Claire was still in Russia. Mary writes:—"I wrote to you last while I entertained the hope that my money cares were diminishing, but shabby as the best of these shabby people was, I am not to arrive at that best without due waiting and anxiety. Nor do I yet see the end of this worse than tedious uncertainty." Mary was to see Shelley's younger brother, who was just married, but she had small hope of reaping any good from his visit. She adds, "Adieu, my ever dear friend; while hearts such as yours beat, I will not wholly despond." Mary refers with great kindness to Hunt, and is most anxious as to his future. She also notices with high satisfaction that the Whigs with Canning are in the ascendant, and that they may be favourable to Greece. While Mary Shelley was residing in Kentish Town, before she joined her father in Gower Place after the winding up of his affairs, a letter from Godwin to his wife at the sea-side shows that the latter considered he did not need her society as Mrs. Shelley was with him; he explains that he sees her about twice a week, but is feeling lonely every day.

After Mary removed to Gower Place in 1827, among other work, she was occupied by her *Lives of Eminent Literary Men*, for *Lardner's Cyclopædia*. About the same year Godwin writes to his daughter who is evidently in very low spirits, wishing that she resembled him in temperament rather than the Wollstonecrafts, but explains that his present good spirits may be owing to his work on Cromwell. A little later we find Godwin writing to Mary, himself in depression. He is troubled by publishers who will not decide to take a novel. "Three, four, or five hundred pounds, and to be subsisted by them while I write it," is what he hoped to get. Mrs. Shelley was at Southend for change of air, and wishing her father to join her; but this he could not decide on. Every day lost is taking away from his means of subsistence; for he is writing now, not for marble to be placed over his remains, but for bread to be put into his mouth.

In April 1829, Mrs. Shelley, writing still from her father's address, 44, Grower Street, complains to Trelawny in a truly English way, as she says, of the weather. She rejoices that her friend has taken to work, and hopes that his friends will keep him to recording his own adventures; but she strongly dissuades him from writing a life of Shelley, for how could that be done without bringing her into publicity? which she shrinks from fearfully, though she is forced by her hard situation to meet it in a thousand ways; or as she expresses it, "I will tell you what I am, a silly goose, who, far from wishing to stand forward to assert myself in any way, now that I am alone in the world have but the desire to wrap night and the obscurity of insignificance around me. This is weakness, but I cannot help it." Neither does Mary consider that the time has come to write Shelley's life, though she her-self hopes to do so some day.

Towards the end of 1830 we find Mary in Somerset Street, Portman Square, from which place she writes to Trelawny on the subject of his MS. of *The Adventures of a Younger Son*, which he had consigned to her hands to place with a publisher, make the best terms for that she could, and see through the press; a task distasteful to Trelawny to the last. Mrs. Shelley much admired the work, considering it full of passion and interest. But she does not hesitate to point out the blemishes, certain coarsenesses, which she begs him to allow her to deal with, as she would have dealt with parts of Lord Byron's *Don Juan*. She is sure that without this she will have great difficulty in disposing of the book.

Mary finds the absorbing politics of the day a great hindrance to publishing, and says: "God knows how it will all end, but it looks as if the aristocrats would have the good sense to make the necessary sacrifices to a starving population."

The worry of awaiting the decision of the publisher was felt by Mrs. Shelley more for Trelawny than for herself; she finds it difficult to make the terms she wishes for him, and, writing to her friend on March 22 of the next year, she regrets that she cannot make Colburn, the best publisher she knows of, give five hundred pounds as she wishes, but trusts to get three hundred pounds for first edition and two hundred pounds for second; but times have changed since she first returned to England, neither she nor her father can command the same prices which they did then. At that time "publishers came to seek me," she writes; "now money is scarcer and readers fewer than ever."

Three days later she is able to add the news that she has received "the ultimatum of these great people," three hundred pounds down and one hundred pounds on second edition, she thinks, for 1,000 copies. She advises acceptance, but will try other publishers if he wish it.

Mary again regrets that it is impossible for her to go to Italy. She expresses herself as wretched in England, and in spite of her sanguine disposition and capacity to endure, which have borne her up hitherto, she feels sinking at last; situated as she is, it is impossible for her not to be wretched.

Mary does not give way long to despondency, she goes on to tell news as to Medwin, Hogg, Jane, &c.; she can even tease Trelawny about the different ladies who believe themselves the sole object of his affection, and tells him she is having a certain letter of his about "Caroline" lithographed, and thinks of dispensing 100 copies among "the many hapless fair."

A third letter on the subject of the book, on June 14, 1831, tells Trelawny how his work is in progress, and Horace Smith, who much admires it, has promised to revise it. Again, in July of the same year, she writes that the third volume is in print, and his book will soon be published; but that as his mother talks openly of his memoirs in society, he must not hope for secrecy. In this letter, also, we have a fact which redounds to the credit of both Mary Shelley and Trelawny, as she clearly tells him she cannot marry him; but remains in "all gratitude and friendship" his M. S. Trelawny had evidently made her an offer of marriage, moved perhaps by gratitude for her help, as well as probably, in his case, a passing love; for she writes to him: "My name will never be Trelawny. I am not so young as I was when you first knew me, but I am as proud. I must have the entire affection, devotion, and, above all, the solicitous protection of any one who would win me. You belong to womenkind in general, and Mary S. will *never* be yours. I write in haste," &c. &c.

Trelawny would never have offered his name thus to a woman he could not respect, and perhaps few know better than those of his reckless class who are most worthy of respect. Mary Shelley, who dreaded men's looks or words, by her own knowledge and her intimate friends' accounts had no fear of him; he had the instincts of a gentleman for a true lady, who may be found in any class.

Four years later, we have Mary again writing to Mr. Trelawny with regard to his book, a second edition being called for, when, to her confusion, she finds that through her not having read over the agreement, and having taken for granted that the proposal of three hundred pounds on first edition with one hundred pounds more on second was inserted, she had signed the contract; but now it turned out that what was proposed by letter was not inserted by Oilier in the agreement, and she knew not what to do. In a second letter a few days later from Harrow, where she lived for a while to be near her son at school, she wrote in answer to Trelawny, proposing Peacock as umpire, because, she writes, "he would not lean to the strongest side, which Jefferson, as a lawyer, is inclined, I think, to do." Oilier, she writes, devoutly wished she had read the agreement, as the clause ought to have been in it.

Again, a few months later, on April 7, 1836, there is another letter asking Trelawny if he would like to attend her father's funeral, and if he would go with the undertaker to choose the spot nearest to her mother's, in St. Pancras

Churchyard, and, if he could do this, to write to Mrs. Godwin, at the Exchequer, to tell her so. The last few years of Godwin's life had not ended, as he had so bitterly apprehended, in penury; as his friends in power had obtained for him the post of Yeoman Usher of the Exchequer, with residence in New Palace Yard, in 1833. The office was in fact a sinecure, and was soon abolished; but it was arranged that no change should be made in the old philosopher's position. His old friends had died, but his work had its reward for him, as well as its place in the thought of the world, for such people as the Duke of Wellington and Lord Melbourne had used their influence for him. Mary had been his constant devoted daughter to the last. In 1834 he writes to his wife of Mrs. Shelley, as he always called his daughter to Mrs. Godwin, of various meetings and dinners with each other, though he cannot attend her evenings as he would wish, since the walk across the park to reach Somerset Street, where she then lived, was by no means pleasant after dark: and now we find Mary honouring Trelawny with the last service for her father, apologising, but adding, "Are you not the best and most constant of friends?"

Godwin's last grief was the loss of his son. William in 1832; he had been settled in a literary career and left a widow. One of Mary's first acts of generosity later on was to settle a pension on her.

CHAPTER XIV.

LITERARY WORK.

Having traced Mary's life, as far as space will allow, to the death of her father, we must now retrace our steps to show the work she did, which gives the *raison-d'être* for this biography. It has already been shown that her second book, *Valperga*, much admired by Shelley, was written to assist her father in his distress before his bankruptcy. After her husband's death, while arranging his MSS., and noting facts in connection with them, she planned and wrote her third romance, *The Last Man*.

This highly imaginative work of Mary Shelley's twenty-sixth year contains some of the author's most powerful ideas; but is marred in the commencement by some of her most stilted writing.

The account of the events recorded professes to be found in the cave of the Cumsean Sibyl, near Naples, where they had remained for centuries, outlasting the changes of nature and, when found, being still two hundred and fifty years in advance of the time foretold. The accounts are all written on the sibylline leaves; they are in all languages, ancient and modern; and those concerning this story are in English.

We find ourselves in England, in 2073, in the midst of a Republic, the last king of England having abdicated at the quietly expressed wish of his subjects. This book, like all Mrs. Shelley's, is full of biographical reminiscences; the introduction gives the date of her own visit to Naples with Shelley, in 1818; the places they visited are there indicated; the poetry, romance, the pleasures and pains of her own existence, are worked into her subjects; while her imagination carries her out of her own surroundings. We clearly recognise in the ideal character of the son of the abdicated king an imaginary portrait of Shelley as Mary would have him known, not as she knew him as a living person. To give an adequate idea of genius with all its charm, and yet with its human imperfections, was beyond Mary's power. Adrian, the son of kings, the aristocratic republican, is the weakest part, and one cannot help being struck by Mary Shelley's preference for the aristocrat over the plebeian. In fact, Mary's idea of a republic still needed kings' sons by their good manners to grace it, while, at the same time, the king's son had to be transmuted into an ideal Shelley. This strange confusion of ideas allowed for, and the fact that over half a century of perhaps the earth's most rapid period of progress has passed, the imaginative qualities are still remarkable in Mary. Balloons, then dreamed of, were attained; but naturally the steam-engine and other wonders of science, now achieved, were unknown to Mary. When the plague breaks out she has scope for her fancy, and she certainly adds vivid pictures of horror and pathos to a subject which has been handled by masters of thought at different periods. In this time of horror it is amusing to note how the people's candidate, Ryland, represented as a vulgar specimen of humanity, succumbs to abject fear. The description of the deserted towns and grass-grown streets of London is impressive. The fortunes of the family, to whom the last man, Lionel Verney, belongs, are traced through their varying phases, as one by one the dire plague assails them, and Verney, the only man who recovers from the disease, becomes the leader of the remnant of the English nation. This small handful of humanity leaves England, and wanders through France on its way to the favoured southern countries where human aid, now so scarce, was less needed. On this journey Mrs. Shelley avails herself of reminiscences of her own travelling with Shelley some few years before; and we pass the places noted in her diary; but strange grotesque figures cross the path of the few wanderers, who are decimated each day. At one moment a dying acrobat, deserted by his companions, is seen bounding in the air behind a hedge in the dusk of evening. At another, a black figure mounted on a horse, which only shows itself after dark, to cause apprehensions soon calmed by the death of the poor wanderer, who wished only for distant companionship through dread of contagion. Dijon is reached and passed, and here the old Countess of Windsor, the ex-Queen of England, dies: she had only been reconciled to her changed position by the destruction of humanity. Once, near Geneva, they come upon the sound of divine music in a church, and find a dying girl playing to her blind father to keep up the delusion to the last. The small party, reduced by this time to five, reach Chamouni, and the grand scenes so familiar to Mary contrast with the final tragedy of the human race; yet one more dies, and only four of one family remain; they bury the dead man in an ice cavern, and with this last victim find the pestilence has ended, after a seven years' reign over the earth. A weight is lifted from the atmosphere, and the world is before them; but now alone they must visit her ruins; and the beauty of the earth and the love of each other, bear them up till none but the last man remains to complete the Cumsæan Sibyl's prophecy.

Various stories of minor importance followed from Mrs. Shelley's pen, and preparations were made for the lives of eminent literary men. But it was not till the year preceding her father's death that we have *Lodore*, published in 1835. Of this novel we have already spoken in relation to the separation of Shelley and Harriet.

Mary had too much feeling of art in her work to make an imaginary character a mere portrait, and we are constantly reminded in her novels of the different wonderful and interesting personages whom she knew intimately, though most of their characters were far too subtle and complex to be unravelled by her, even with her intimate knowledge. Indeed, the very fact of having known some of the greatest people of her age, or of almost any age, gives an appearance of affectation to her novels, as it fills them with characters so far from the common run that their place in life cannot be reduced to an ordinary fashionable level. Romantic episodes there may be, but their true place is in the theatre of time of which they are the movers, not the Lilliputians of life who are slowly worked on and moulder by them, and whose small doings are the material of most novels. We know of few novelists who have touched at all successfully on the less known characters. This accomplishment seems to need the great poet himself.

The manner in which Lady Lodore is influenced seems to point to Harriet; but the unyielding and revengeful side of her character has certainly more of Lady Byron. She is charmingly described, and shows a great deal of insight on Mary's part into the life of fashionable people of her time, which then, perhaps more than now, was the favourite theme with novelists. This must be owing to a certain innate Tory propensity in the English classes or masses for whom Mary Shelley had to work hard, and for whose tendencies in this respect she certainly had a sympathy. Mary's own life, at the point we have now reached, is also here touched on in the character of Ethel, Lord and Lady Lodore's daughter, who is brought up in America by her father, and on his death entrusted to an aunt, with injunctions in his will that she is not to be allowed to be brought in contact with her mother. Her character is sweetly feminine and trusting, and in her fortunate love and marriage (in all but early money matters) might be considered quite unlike Mary's own less fortunate experiences; but in her perfect love and confidence in her husband, her devotion and unselfishness through the trials of poverty in London, the descriptions of which were evidently taken from Mary's own experiences, there is no doubt of the resemblance, as also in her love and reverence for all connected with her father. There are also passages undoubtedly expressive of her own inner feelings—such as this when describing the young husband and wife at a *tête-à-tête* supper:—

Mutual esteem and gratitude sanctified the unreserved sympathy which made each so happy in the other. Did they love the less for not loving "in sin and fear"? Far from it. The certainty of being the cause of good to each other tended to foster the most delicate of all passions, more than the rough ministrations of terror and the knowledge that each was the occasion of injury. A woman's heart is peculiarly unfitted to sustain this conflict. Her sensibility gives keenness to her imagination and she magnifies every peril, and writhes beneath every sacrifice which tends to humiliate her in her own eyes. The natural pride of her sex struggles with her desire to confer happiness, and her peace is wrecked.

What stronger expression of feeling could be needed than this, of a woman speaking from her heart and her own experiences? Does it not remind one of the moral on this subject in all George Eliot's writing, where she shows that the outcome of what by some might be considered minor transgressions against morality leads even in modern times to the Nemesis of the most terrible Greek Dramas?

The complicated money transactions carried on with the aid of lawyers were clearly a reminiscence of Shelley's troubles, and of her own incapacity to feel all the distress contingent so long as she was with him, and there was evidently money somewhere in the family, and it would come some time. In this novel we also perceive that Mary works off her pent-up feelings with regard to Emilia Viviani. It cannot be supposed that the corporeal part of Shelley's creation of *Epipsychidion* (so exquisite in appearance and touching in manner and story as to give rise, when transmitted through the poet's brain, to the most perfect of love ideals) really ultimately became the fiery-tempered worldly-minded virago that Mary Shelley indulges herself in depicting, after first, in spite of altering some relations and circumstances, clearly showing whom the character was intended for. It is true that Shelley himself, after investing her with divinity to serve the purposes of art, speaks later of her as a very commonplace worldly-minded woman; but poets, like artists, seem at times to need lay figures to attire with their thoughts. Enough has been shown to prove that there is genuine subject of interest in this work of Mary's thirty-seventh year.

The next work, *Falkner*, published in 1837, is the last novel we have by Mary Shelley; and as we see from her letter she had been passing through a period of ill-health and depression while writing it, this may account for less spontaneity in the style, which is decidedly more stilted; but, here again, we feel that we are admitted to some of the circle which Mary had encountered in the stirring times of her life, and there is undoubted imagination with some fine descriptive passages.

The opening chapter introduces a little deserted child in a picturesque Cornish village. Her parents had died there in apartments, one after the other, the husband having married a governess against the wishes of his relations; consequently, the wife was first neglected on her husband's death; and on her own sudden death, a few months later, the child was simply left to the care of the poor people of the village—a dreamy, poetic little thing, whose one pleasure was to stroll in the twilight to the village churchyard and be with her mamma. Here she was found by Falkner, the principal character of the romance, who had selected this very spot to end a ruined existence; in which attempt he was frustrated by the child jogging his arm to move him from her mother's grave. His life being thus saved by the child's instrumentality, he naturally became interested in her. He is allowed to look through the few remaining papers of the parents. Among these he finds an unfinished letter of the wife, evidently addressed to a lady he had known, and also indications who the parents were. He was much moved, and offered to relieve the poor people of the child and to restore her to her relations.

The mother's unfinished letter to her friend contains the following passage, surely autobiographical:—

When I lost Edwin (the husband), I wrote to Mr. Raby (the husband's father) acquainting him with the sad intelligence, and asking for a maintenance for myself and my child. The family solicitor answered my letter. Edwin's conduct had, I was told, estranged his family from him, and they could only regard me as one encouraging his disobedience and apostasy. I had no claim on them. If my child were sent to them, and I would promise to abstain from all intercourse with her, she should be brought up with her cousins, and treated in all respects like one of the family. I declined their barbarous offer, and haughtily and in few words relinquished every claim on their bounty, declaring my intention to support and bring up my child myself. This was foolishly done, I fear; but I cannot regret it, even now.

I cannot regret the impulse that made me disdain these unnatural and cruel relatives, or that led me to take my poor orphan to my heart with pride as being all my own. What had they done to merit such a treasure? And did they show themselves capable of replacing a fond and anxious mother? This reminds the reader of the correspondence between Mary and her father on Shelley's death.

It suffices to say that Falkner became so attached to the small child, that by the time he discovered her relations he had not the heart to confide her to their hard guardianship, and as he was compelled to leave England shortly, he took her with him, and through all difficulties he contrived that she should be well guarded and brought up. There is much in the character of Falkner that reminds the reader of Trelawny, the gallant and generous friend of Byron and Shelley in their last years, the brave and romantic traveller. The description of Falkner's face and figure must have much resembled that of Trelawny when young, though, of course, the incidents of the story have no connection with him. In the meantime the little girl is growing up, and the nurses are replaced by an English governess, whom Falkner engages abroad, and whose praises and qualifications he hears from everyone at Odessa. The story progresses through various incidents foreshadowing the cause of Falkner's mystery. Elizabeth, the child, now grown up, passes under his surname. While travelling in Germany they come across a youth of great personal attraction, who appears, however, to be of a singularly reckless and misanthropical disposition for one so young. Elizabeth seeming attracted by his daring and beauty, Falkner suddenly finds it necessary to return to England. Shortly afterwards, he is moved to go to Greece during the War of Independence, and wishes to leave Elizabeth with her relations in England;

but this she strenuously opposes so far as to induce Falkner to let her accompany him to Greece, where he places her with a family while he rushes into the thick of the danger, only hoping to end his life in a good cause. In this he nearly succeeds, but Elizabeth, hearing of his danger, hastens to his side, and nurses him assiduously through the fever brought on from his wounds and the malarious climate. By short stages and the utmost care, she succeeds in reaching Malta on their homeward journey, and Falkner, a second time rescued from death by his beloved adopted child, determines not again to endanger recklessly the life more dear to her than that of many fathers. Again, at Malta, during a fortnight's quarantine, the smallness of the world of fashionable people brings them in contact with an English party, a Lord and Lady Cecil, who are travelling with their family. Falkner is too ill to see anyone, and when Elizabeth finally gets him on board a vessel to proceed to Genoa, he seems rapidly sinking. In his despair and loneliness, feeling unable to cope with all the difficulties of burning sun and cold winds, help unexpectedly comes: a gentleman whom Elizabeth has not before perceived, and whom now she is too much preoccupied to observe, quietly arranges the sail to shelter the dying man from sun and wind, places pillows, and does all that is possible; he even induces the poor girl to go below and rest on a couch for a time while he watches. Falkner becomes easier in the course of the night; he sleeps and gains in strength, and from this he progresses till, while at Marseilles, he hears the name, Neville, of the unknown friend who had helped to restore him to life. He becomes extremely agitated and faints. On being restored to consciousness he begs Elizabeth to continue the journey with him alone, as he can bear no one but her near him. The mystery of Falkner's life seems to be forcing itself to the surface.

The travellers reach England, and Elizabeth is sought out by Lady Cecil, who had been much struck by her devotion to her father. Elizabeth is invited to stay with Lady Cecil, as she much needs rest in her turn. During a pleasant time of repose near Hastings, Elizabeth hears Lady Cecil talk much of her brother Gerard; but it is not till he, too, arrives on a visit, that she acknowledges to herself that he is really the same Mr. Neville whom she had met, and from whom she had received such kindness. Nor had Gerard spoken of Elizabeth; he had been too much drawn towards her, as his life also is darkened by a mystery. They spend a short tranquil time together, when a letter announces the approaching arrival of Sir Boyvill Neville, the young man's father (although Lady Cecil called Gerard her brother, they were not really related; Sir Boyvill had married the mother of Lady Cecil, who was the offspring of a previous marriage).

Gerard Neville at once determines to leave the house, but before going refers Elizabeth to his sister, Lady Cecil, to hear the particulars of the tragedy which surrounds him. The story told is this. Sir Boyvill Neville was a man of the world with all the too frequent disbelief in women and selfishness. This led to his becoming very tyrannical when he married, at the age of 45, Alethea, a charming young woman who had recently lost her mother, and whose father, a retired naval officer of limited means, would not hear of her refusing so good an offer as Sir Boyvill's. After their marriage Sir Boyvill, feeling himself too fortunate in having secured so charming and beautiful a wife, kept out of all society, and after living abroad for some years took her to an estate he possessed in Cumberland. They lived there shut out from all the world, except for trips which he took himself to London, or elsewhere, whenever *ennui* assailed him. They had, at the time we are approaching, two charming children, a beautiful boy of some ten years and a little girl of two. At this time while Alethea was perfectly happy with her children, and quite contented with her retirement, which she perceived took away the jealous tortures of her husband, he left home for a week, drawn out to two months, on one of his periodical visits to the capital. Lady Neville's frequent letters concerning her home and her children were always cheerful and placid, and the time for her husband's return was fixed. He arrived at the appointed hour in the evening. The servants were at the door to receive him, but in an instant alarm prevailed; Lady Neville and her son Gerard were not with him. They had left the house some hours before to walk in the park, and had not since been seen or heard of, an unprecedented occurrence. The alarm was raised; the country searched in all directions, but ineffectually, during a fearful tempest. Ultimately the poor boy was found unconscious on the ground, drenched to the skin. On his being taken home, and his father questioning him, all that could be heard were his cries "Come back, mamma; stop, stop for me!" Nothing else but the tossings of fever. Once again, "Then she has come back," he cried, "that man did not take her quite away; the carriage drove here at last." The story slowly elicited from the child on his gaining strength was this. On his going for a walk with his mother in the park, she took the key of a gate which led into a lane. A gentleman was waiting outside. Gerard had never seen him before, but he heard his mother call him Rupert. They walked together through the lane accompanied by the child, and talked earnestly. She wept, and the boy was indignant. When they reached a cross-road, a carriage was waiting. On approaching it the gentleman pulled the child's hands from hers, lifted her in, sprang in after, and the coachman drove like the wind, leaving the child to hear his mother shriek in agony, "My child—my son!" Nothing more could be discovered; the country was ransacked in vain. The servants only stated that ten days ago a gentleman called, asked for Lady Neville and was shown in to her; he remained some two hours, and on his leaving it was remarked that she had been weeping. He had called again but was not admitted. One letter was found, signed "Rupert," begging for one more meeting, and if that were granted he would leave her and his just revenge for ever; otherwise, he could not tell what the consequences might be on her husband's return that night. In answer to this letter she went, but with her child, which clearly proved her innocent intention. Months passed with no fresh result, till her husband, beside himself with wounded pride, determined to be avenged by obtaining a Bill of Divorce in the House of Lords, and producing his son Gerard as evidence against his lost mother, whom he so dearly loved. The poor child by this time, by dint of thinking and weighing every word he could remember, such as "I grieve deeply for you, Rupert: my good wishes are all I have to give you," became more and more convinced that his mother was taken forcibly away, and would return at any moment if she were able. He only longed for the time when he should be old enough to go and seek her through the world. His father was relentless, and the child was brought before the House of Lords to repeat the evidence he had innocently given against her; but when called on to speak in that awful position, no word could be drawn from him except "She is innocent." The House was moved by the brave child's agony, and resolved to carry on the case without him, from the witnesses whom he had spoken to, and finally they pronounced a decree of divorce in Sir Boyvill's favour. The struggle and agony of the poor child are admirably described, as also his subsequent flight from his father's house, and wanderings round his old home in Cumberland. In his fruitless search for his mother he reached a deserted sea-coast. After wandering about for two months barefoot, and almost starving but for the ewe's milk and bread given him by the cottagers, he was recognized. His father, being informed, had him seized and brought home, where he was confined and treated as a criminal. His state became so helpless that even his father was at length moved to some feeling of self-restraint, and finally took Gerard with him abroad, where he was first seen at Baden by Elizabeth and Palkner. There also he first met his sister by affinity, Lady Cecil. With her he lost somewhat his defiant tone, and felt that for his mother's sake he must not appear to others as lost in sullenness and despair. He now talked of his mother, and reasoned about her; but although he much interested Lady Cecil, he did not convince her really of his mother's innocence, so much did all circumstances weigh against her. But now, during Elizabeth's visit to Lady Cecil, a letter is received by Gerard and his father informing them that one Gregory Hoskins believed he could give some information; he was at Lancaster. Sir Boyvill, only anxious to hush up the matter by which his pride had suffered, hastened to prevent his son from taking steps to re-open the subject. This Hoskins was originally a native of the district round Dromoor, Neville's home, and had emigrated to America at the time of Sir Boyvill's marriage. At one time—years ago—he met a man named Osborne, who confided to him how he had gained money before coming to America by helping a gentleman to carry off a lady, and how terribly the affair ended, as the lady got drowned in a river near which they had placed her while nearly dead from fright, on the dangerous coast of Cumberland. On returning to

England, and hearing the talk about the Nevilles in his native village, this old story came to his mind, and he wrote his letter. Neville, on hearing this, instantly determined to proceed to Mexico, trace out Osborne, and bring him to accuse his mother's murderer.

All these details were written by Elizabeth to her beloved father. After some delay, one line entreated her to come to him instantly for one day.

Falkner could not ignore the present state of things—the mutual attraction of his Elizabeth and of Gerard. Yet how, with all he knew, could that be suffered to proceed? Never, except by eternal separation from his adored child; but this should be done. He would now tell her his story. He could not speak, but he wrote it, and now she must come and receive it from him. He told of all his solitary, unloved youth, the miseries and tyranny of school to the unprotected—a reminiscence of Shelley; how, on emerging from, childhood, one gleam of happiness entered his life in the friendship of a lady, an old friend of his mother's, who had one lovely daughter; of the happy, innocent time spent in their cottage during holidays; of the dear lady's death; of her daughter's despair; then how he was sent off to India; of letters he wrote to the daughter Alethea, letters unanswered, as the father, the naval officer, intercepted all; of his return, after years, to England, his one hope that which had buoyed him up through years of constancy, to meet and marry his only love, for that he felt she was and must remain. He recounted his return, and the news lie received; his one rash visit to her to judge for himself whether she was happy—this, from her manner, he could not feel, in spite of her delight in her children; his mad request to see her; mad plot, and still madder execution of it, till he had her in his arms, dashing through the country, through storm and thunder, unable to tell whether she lived or died; the first moment of pause; the efforts to save the ebbing life in a ruined hut; the few minutes' absence to seek materials for fire; the return, to find her a floating corpse in the wild little river flowing to the sea; the rescue of her body from the waves; her burial on the sea-shore; and his own subsequent life of despair, saved twice by Elizabeth. All this was told to the son, to whom Falkner denounced himself as his mother's destroyer. He named the spot where the remains would be found. And now what was left to be done? Only to wait a little, while Sir Boyvill and Gerard Neville proved his words, and traced out the grave. An inquest was held, and Falkner apprehended. A few days passed, and then Elizabeth found her father gone; and by degrees it was broken to her that he was in Carlisle gaol on the charge of murder. She, who had not feared the dangers in Greece of war and fever, was not to be deterred now; she, who believed in his innocence. No minutes were needed to decide her to go straight to Carlisle, and remain as near as she could to the dear father who had rescued and cared for her when deserted. Gerard, who was with his father when the bones were exhumed at the spot indicated, soon realised the new situation. His passion for justice to his mother did not deaden his feeling for others. He felt that Falkner's story was true, and though nothing could restore his mother's life, her honour was intact. Sir Boyvill would leave no stone unturned to be revenged, rightly or wrongly, on the man who had assailed his domestic peace; but Gerard saw Elizabeth, gave what consolation he could, and determined to set off at once to America to seek Osborne, as the only witness who could exculpate Falkner from the charge of murder. After various difficulties Osborne was found in England, where he had returned in terror of being taken in America as accomplice in the murder. With great difficulty he is brought to give evidence, for all his thoughts and fears are for himself; but at length, when all hopes seem failing, he is induced by Elizabeth to give his evidence, which fully confirms Falkner's statement.

At length the day of trial came. The news of liberty arrived. "Not Guilty!" Who can imagine the effect but those who have passed innocently through the ordeal? Once more all are united. Gerard has to remain for the funeral of his father, who had died affirming his belief, which in fact he had always entertained, in Falkner's innocence. Lady Cecil had secured for Elizabeth the companionship of Mrs. Raby, her relation on the father's side. She takes Falkner and Elizabeth home to the beautiful ancestral Belleforest. Here a time of rest and happiness ensues. Those so much tried by adversity would not let real happiness escape for a chimera; honour being restored love and friendship remained, and Gerard, Elizabeth and Falkner felt that now they ought to remain, together, death not having disunited them. Too much space may appear to be here given to one romance; but it seems just to show the scope of Mary's imaginative conception. There are certainly both imagination and power in carrying it out. It is true that the idea seems founded, to some extent, on Godwin's Caleb Williams, the man passing through life with a mystery; the similar names of Falkner and Falkland may even be meant to call attention to this fact. The three-volume form, in this as in many novels, seems to detract from the strength of the work in parts, the second volume being noticeably drawn out here and there. It may be questioned, also, whether the form adopted in this as in many romances of giving the early history by way of narrative told by one of the *dramatis personæ* to another, is the desirable one—a point to which we have already adverted in relation to *Frankenstein*. Can it be true to nature to make one character give a description, over a hundred pages long, repeating at length, word for word, long conversations which he has never heard, marking the changes of colour which he has not seen—and all this with a minuteness which even the firmest memory and the most loquacious tongue could not recall? Does not this give an unreality to the style incompatible with art, which ought to be the mainspring of all imaginative work? This, however, is not Mrs. Shelley's error alone, but is traceable through many masterpieces. The author, the creator, who sees the workings of the souls of his characters, has, naturally, memory and perception for all. Yet Mary Shelley, in this as in most of her work, has great insight into character. Elizabeth's grandfather in his dotage is quite a photograph from life; old Oswig Raby, who was more shrivelled with narrowness of mind than with age, but who felt himself and his house, the oldest in England, of more importance than aught else he knew of. His daughter-in-law, the widow of his eldest son, is also well drawn; a woman of upright nature who can acknowledge the faults of the family, and try to retrieve them, and who finally does her best to atone for the past.

CHAPTER XV.

LATER WORKS.

The writing of these novels, with other literary work we must refer to, passed over the many years of Mrs. Shelley's life until 1837, and saved her from the ennui of a quiet life in London with few friends. Certainly in Mary's case there had been a reason for the neglect of "Society," which at times she bitterly deplored; and as she had little other than intellectual and amiable qualities to recommend her for many years, she was naturally not sought after by the more successful of her contemporaries. There are instances even of her being cruelly mortified by marked rudeness at some receptions she attended; in one case years later, when her fidelity to her husband and his memory might have appeased the sternest moralist. During these early years, which she writes of afterwards as years of privation which caused her to shed many bitter tears at the time, though they were frequently gilded by imagination, Mrs. Shelley was cheered by seeing her son grow up entirely to her satisfaction, passing through the child's stage and the school-boy's at Harrow, from which place he proceeded to Cambridge; and many and substantially happy years must have been passed, during which Claire was not forgotten. Poor Claire, who passed through much severe servitude, from which Mary would fain have spared her, as she wrote once to Mr. Trelawny that this was one of her chief reasons for wishing for independence; but "Old Time," or "Eternity," as she called Sir Timothy, who certainly had no reason to claim her affection, was long in passing; and though a small allowance before 1831 of three hundred pounds a year had increased to four hundred pounds a year when her only child reached his majority in 1841, for this, on Sir Timothy's death, she had to repay thirteen thousand pounds. It had enabled her to make a tour in Germany with her son; of this journey we will speak after referring to her *Lives of Eminent Literary Men.*

These lives, written for *Lardner's Cyclopedia*, and published in 1835, are a most interesting series of biographies written by a woman who could appreciate the poet's character, and enter into the injustices and sorrows from which few poets have been exempt. They show careful study, her knowledge of various countries gives local colour to her descriptions, and her love of poetry makes her an admirable critic. She is said to have written all the Italian and Spanish lives with the exception of Galileo and Tasso; and certainly her writing contrasts most favourably with the life of Tasso, to whomever this may have been assigned. Mary was much disappointed at not having this particular sketch to write.

To her life of Dante she affixes Byron's lines from *The Prophecy of Dante—*

'Tis the doom
Of spirits of my order to be racked
In life; to wear their hearts out, and consume
Their days in endless strife, and die alone.
Then future thousands crowd around their tomb,
And pilgrims, come from climes where they have known
The name of him who now is but a name,
Spread his, by him unheard, unheeded fame.

Mary felt how these beautiful lines were appropriate to more than one poet. Freedom from affectation, and a genuine love of her subject, make her biographies most readable, and for the ordinary reader there is a fund of information. The next life—that of Petrarch—is equally attractive; in fact, there is little that can exceed the interest of lives of these immortal beings when written—with the comprehension here displayed. Even the complicated history of the period is made clear, and the poet, whose tortures came from the heart, is as feelingly touched on as he who suffered from the political factions of the Bianchi and the Neri, and who felt the steepness of other's stairs and the salt savour of other's bread. Petrarch's banishment through love is not less feelingly described, and we are taken to the life and the homes of the time in the living descriptions given by Mary. One passage ought in fairness to be given to show her enthusiastic understanding and appreciation of the poet she writes of:—

Dante, as hath been already intimated, is the hero of his own poem; and the Divina Commedia is the only example of an attempt triumphantly achieved, and placed beyond the reach of scorn or neglect, wherein from beginning to end the author discourses concerning himself individually. Had this been done in any other way than the consummately simple, delicate, and unobtrusive one which he has adopted, the whole would have been insufferable egotism, disgusting coxcombry, or oppressive dulness. Whereas, this personal identity is the charm, the strength, the soul of the book; he lives, he breathes, he moves through it; his pulse beats or stands still, his eye kindles or fades, his cheek grows pale with horror, colours with shame, or burns with indignation; we hear his voice, his step, in every page; we see his shape by the flame of hell; his shadow in the land where there is no *other* shadow (*Purgatoria*) and his countenance gaining angelic elevation from "colloquy sublime" with glorified intelligence in the paradise above. Nor does he ever go out of his natural character. He is, indeed, the lover from infancy of Beatrice, the aristocratic magistrate of a fierce democracy, the valiant soldier in the field of Campaldino, the fervent patriot in the feuds of Guelphs and Ghibellines, the eloquent and subtle disputant in the school of theology, the melancholy exile wandering from court to court, depending for bread and shelter on petty princes who knew not his worth, except as a splendid captive in their train; and above all, he is the poet anticipating his own assured renown (though not obtrusively so), and dispensing at his will honour or infamy to others, whom he need but to name, and the sound must be heard to the end of time and echoed from all regions of the globe. Dante in his vision is Dante as he lived, as he died, and as he expected to live in both worlds beyond death—an immortal spirit in the one, an unforgotten poet in the other.

You feel this is written from the heart of the woman who herself felt as she wrote. We would fain go through her different biographies, tracing her feelings, her appreciation, and poetic enthusiasm throughout, but that is impossible. She takes us through Boccaccio's life, and, as by the reflection of a sunset from a mirror, we are warmed with the glow and mirth from distant and long-past times in Italy. One feels through her works the innate delicacy of her mind. Through Boccaccio's life, as through all the others, the history of the times and the noteworthy facts concerning the poets are brought forward—such as the sums of money Boccaccio spent, though poor, to promote the study of Greek, so long before the taking of Constantinople by the Turks. In the friendship of Petrarch and Boccaccio, she shows how great souls can love, and makes you love them in return, and you feel the riches of the meetings of such people, these dictators of mankind—not of a faction-tossed country or continent. How paltry do the triumphs of conquerors which end with the night, the feasts of princes which leave still hungry, appear beside the triumphs of intellect, the symposium of souls.

After Boccaccio, Mary rapidly ran over the careers of Lorenzo de' Medici, Ficino, Pico della Mirandola, Politian, and the Pulci, exhibiting again, after the lapse of a century, the study in Italy of the Greek language. The story of the truly great prince with his circle of poet friends, one of whom, Politian, died of a broken heart at the death of his beloved patron, is well told. From these she passes on to the followers of the romantic style begun by Pulci, Cieco da Ferrara, Burchiello, Bojardo; then Berni, born at the end of the fifteenth century, who carried on or recast Bojardo's *Orlando Innamorato*, which was followed by Ariosto's *Orlando Furioso*, the delight of Italy. In Ariosto's life Mary, as ever, delights in showing the filial affection and fine traits of the poet's nature. She quotes his lines—

Our mother's years with pity fill my heart,
For without infamy she could not be
By all of us at once forsaken.

But with these commendations she strongly denounces the profligacy of his writing as presumably of his life. She says: "An author may not be answerable to posterity for the evil of his mortal life; but for the profligacy of that life which he lives through after ages, contaminating by irrepressible and incurable infection the minds of others, he is amenable even in his grave."

Through the intricacies of Machiavelli Mary's clear head and conscientious treatment lead the reader till light appears to gleam. The many-sided character of the man comes out, the difficulties of the time he wrote in, while advising Princes how to act in times of danger, and so admonishing the people how to resist. Did he not foresee tyranny worked out and resistance complete, and his own favourite republic succeeding to the death of tyrants? One remark of Mary's with regard to the time when Machiavelli considered himself most neglected is worth recording: "He bitterly laments the inaction of his life, and expresses an ardent desire to be employed. Meanwhile he created occupation for himself, and it is one of the lessons that we may derive from becoming acquainted with the feelings and actions of celebrated men, to learn that this very period during which Machiavelli repined at the neglect of his contemporaries, and the tranquillity of his life, was that during which his fame took root, and which brought his name down to us. He occupied his leisure in writing those works which have occasioned his immortality."

A short life of Guicciardini follows; then Mrs. Shelley comes to the congenial subject of Vittoria Colonna, the noble widow of the Marquis of Pescara, the dear friend in her latter years of Michael Angelo, the woman whose writings, accomplishments, and virtues have made her the pride of Italy. With her Mary Shelley gives a few of the long list of names of women who won fame in Italy from their intellect:—the beautiful daughter of a professor, who lectured behind a veil in Petrarch's time; the mother of Lorenzo de' Medici, Ippolita Sforza; Alessandra Scala; Isotta of Padua; Bianca d'Este; Damigella Torella; Cassandra Fedele. We next pass to the life of Guarini, and missing Tasso, whose life Mary Shelley did not write, we come to Chiabrera, who tried to introduce the form of Greek poetry into Italian. Tassoni, Marini, Filicaja are agreeable, but shortly touched on. Then Metastasio is reached, whose youthful genius as an _improvisatore early gained him applause, which was followed up by his successful writing of three-act dramas for the opera, and a subsequent calm and prosperous life at Vienna, under the successive protection of the Emperor Charles VI., Maria Theresa, and Joseph II. The contrast of the even prosperity of Metastasio's life with that of some of the great poets is striking. Next Goldoni claims attention, whose comedies of Italian manners throw much light upon the frivolous life in society before the French Revolution, his own career adding to the pictures of the time. Then Alfieri's varied life-story is well told, his sad period of youth, when taken from his mother to suffer much educational and other neglect, the difficulties he passed through owing to his Piedmontese origin and consequent ignorance of the pure Italian language. She closes the modern

Italian poets with Monti and Ugo Foscolo, whose sad life in London is exhibited.

Mary's studies in Spanish enabled her to treat equally well the poets of Spain and of Portugal. Her introduction is a good essay on the poetry and poets of Spain, and some of the translations, which are her own, are very happily given. The poetic impulse in Spain is traced from the Iberians through the Romans, Visigoths, Moors, and the early unknown Spanish poets, among whom there were many fine examples. She leads us to Boscan at the commencement of the sixteenth century. Boscan seems to have been one of those rare beings, a poet endowed with all the favours of fortune, including contentment and happiness. His friends Garcilaso di Vega and Mendoza aided greatly in the formation of Spanish poetry, all three having studied the Italian school and Petrarch. This century, rich in poets, gives us also Luis de Leon, Herrera, Saade Miranda, Jorge de Montemayor, Castillejo, the dramatists; and Ercilla, the soldier poet, who, in the expedition for the conquest of Peru went to Arauco, and wrote the poem named *Araucana*. From him we pass to one of the great men of all time, Cervantes, to one who understood the workings of the human heart, and was so much raised above the common level as to be neglected in the magnitude of his own work. Originally of noble family, and having served his country in war, losing his left hand at the battle of Lepanto, he received no recognition of his services after his return from a cruel captivity among the Moors. Instead of reward, Cervantes seems to have met with every indignity that could be devised by the multitudes of pigmies to lower a great man, were that possible. Mary, as ever, rises with her subject. She remarks:—"It is certainly curious that in those days when it was considered part of a noble's duties to protect and patronise men of letters, Cervantes should have been thus passed over; and thus while his book was passing through Europe with admiration, Cervantes remained poor and neglected. So does the world frequently honour its greatest, as if jealous of the renown to which they can never attain."

From Cervantes we pass on to Lope de Vega, of whose thousand dramas what remains? and yet what honours and fortune were showered upon him during his life! A more even balance of qualities enabled him to write entertaining plays, and to flatter the weakness of those in power. From Gongora and Quevedo Mary passes to Calderon, whom she justly considers the master of Spanish poetry. She deplores the little that is known of his life, and that after him the fine period of Spanish literature declines, owing to the tyranny and misrule which were crushing and destroying the spirit and intellect of Spain; for, unfortunately, art and poetry require not only the artist and the poet, but congenial atmosphere to survive in.

Writing for this Cyclopædia was evidently very apposite work for Mrs. Shelley. She wrote also for it lives of some of the French poets. Some stories were also written. In these she was less happy, as likewise in her novel, *Perkin Warbeck*, a pallid imitation of Walter Scott, which does not call for any special comment.

Shortly after her father's death, Mrs. Shelley wrote from 14 North Bank, Regent's Park, to Moxon, wishing to arrange with him about the publication of Godwin's autobiography, letters, &c. But some ten years later we find her still expressing the wish to do some work of the kind as a solemn duty if her health would permit. Probably the very numerous notes which Mrs. Shelley made about her father and his surroundings were towards this object.

Mrs. Shelley's health caused her at times considerable trouble from this period onwards. Harrow had not suited her, and in 1839 she moved to Putney; and the next year, 1840, she was able to make the tour above mentioned, which we cannot do better than refer to at once.

CHAPTER XVI.

ITALY REVISITED.

In Mary Shelley's *Rambles in Germany and Italy* in 1840-42-43, published in 1844, we have not only a pleasing account of herself with her son and friends during a pleasure trip, but some very interesting and charming descriptions of continental life at that time.

Mary, with her son and two college friends, decided in June 1840 to spend their vacation on the banks of the Lake of Como. The idea of again visiting a country where she had so truly lived, and where she had passed through the depths of sorrow, filled her with much emotion. Her failing health made her feel the advantage that travelling and change of country would be to her. After spending an enjoyable two months of the spring at Richmond, visiting Raphael's cartoons at Hampton Court, she went by way of Brighton and Hastings. On her way to Dover she noticed how Hastings, a few years ago a mere fishing village, had then become a new town. They were delayed at Dover by a tempest, but left the next morning, the wind still blowing a gale; reaching Calais they were further delayed by the tide. At length Paris was arrived at, and we find Mary making her first experience at a *table d'hote*. Mary was now travelling with a maid, which no doubt her somewhat weakened health made a necessity to her. They went to the Hotel Chatham at Paris. She felt all the renovating feeling of being in a fresh country out of the little island; the weight of cares seemed to fall from her; the life in Paris cheered her, though the streets were dirty enough then—dirtier than those of London; whereas the contrast is now in the opposite direction.

After a week here they went on towards Como by way of Frankfort. They were to pass Metz, Treves, the Moselle, Coblentz, and the Rhine to Mayence. The freedom from care and, worries in a foreign land, with sufficient means, and only in the company of young people open to enjoyment, gave new life to Mary. After staying a night at Metz, the clean little town on the Moselle, they passed on to Treves. At Thionville, the German frontier, they were struck by the wretched appearance of the cottages in contrast to the French. From Treves they proceeded by boat up the Moselle. The winding banks of the Moselle, with the vineyards sheltered by mountains, are well described. The peasants are content and prosperous, as, after the French Revolution, they bought up the confiscated estates of the nobles, and so were able to cultivate the land. The travellers rowed into the Rhine on reaching Coblentz, and rested at the Bellevue; and now they passed by the grander beauties of the Rhine. These made Mary wish to spend a summer there, exploring its recesses. They reached Mayence at midnight, and the next morning left by rail for Frankfort, the first train they had entered on the Continent. Mary much preferred the comfort of railway travelling. From Frankfort they engaged a voiturier to Schaffhausen, staying at Baden-Baden. The ruined castles recall memories of changed times, and Mary remarks how, except in England and Italy, country houses of the rich seem unknown. At Darmstadt, where they stopped to lunch, they were annoyed and amused too by the inconvenience and inattention they were subjected to from the expected arrival of the Grand Duke. On reaching Heidelberg, she remarks how, in travelling, one is struck by the way that the pride of princes for further dominion causes the devastation of the fairest countries. From the ruined castle they looked over the Palatinate which had been laid waste owing to the ambition of the Princess Elizabeth, daughter of our James I. Mary could have lingered long among the picturesque weed-grown walls, but had to continue the route to their destination. At Baden they visited the gambling saloon, and saw *Rouge et Noir* played. They were much struck by the Falls of the Rhine at Schaffhausen; and, on reaching Chiavenna, Mary had again the delight of hearing and speaking Italian. After crossing the blank mountains, who has not experienced the delight of this sensation has not yet known one of the joys of existence. On arriving at their destination at Lake Como, their temporary resting-place, a passing depression seized the party, the feeling that often comes when shut in by mountains away from home. No doubt Mary having reached Italy, the land she loved, with Shelley, the feeling of being without him assailed her.

At Cadenabia, on Lake Como, they had to consider ways and means. It turned out that apartments, with all their difficulties, would equal hotel expenses without the same amount of comfort. So they decided on accepting the moderate terms offered by the landlord, and were comfortably or even luxuriously installed, with five little bedrooms and large private salon. In one nook of this Mrs. Shelley established her embroidery frame, desk, books, and such things, showing her taste for order and elegance. So for some weeks she and her son and two companions were able to pass their time free from all household worries. The lake and neighbourhood are picturesquely described. One drawback to Mary's peace of mind was the arrival of her son's boat. He seemed to have inherited his father's love of boating, and this naturally filled her with apprehension. They made many pleasant excursions, of which she always gives good descriptions, and also enters clearly into any historical details connected with the country. At times she was carried by the beauty and repose of the scene into rapt moods which she thus describes:—

It has seemed to me, and on such an evening I have felt it, that the world, endowed as it is outwardly with endless shapes and influences of beauty and enjoyment, is peopled also in its spiritual life by myriads of loving spirits, from whom, unaware, we catch impressions which mould our thoughts to good, and thus they guide beneficially the course of events and minister to the destiny of man. Whether the beloved dead make a portion of this holy company, I dare not guess; but that such exist, I feel. They keep far off while we are worldly, evil, selfish; but draw near, imparting the reward of heaven-born joy, when we are animated by noble thoughts and capable of disinterested actions. Surely such gather round me to-night, part of that atmosphere of peace and love which it is paradise to breathe.

I had thought such ecstasy dead in me for ever, but the sun of Italy has thawed the frozen stream.

Such poetic feelings were the natural outcome of the quiet and repose after the life of care and anxiety poor Mary had long been subjected to. She always seems more in her element when describing mountain cataracts, Alpine storms, water lashed into waves and foam by the wind, all the changes of mountain and lake scenery; but this quiet holiday with her son came to an end, and they had to think of turning homewards. Before doing so, they passed by Milan, enjoyed the opera there, and went to see Leonardo da Vinci's "Last Supper," which Mary naturally much admires; she mentions the Luinis without enthusiasm. While here, the non-arrival of a letter caused great anxiety to Mary, as they were now obliged to return on account of Percy's term commencing, and there was barely enough money for him to travel without her; however, that was the only thing possible, and so it had to be done. Percy returned to England with his two friends, and his mother had to remain at Milan awaiting the letter. Days pass without any letter coming to hand, lost days, for Mary was too anxious and worried to be able to take any pleasure in her stay. Nor had she any acquaintances in the place; she could scarcely endure to go down alone to *table d'hôte* dinner, although she overcame this feeling as it was her only time of seeing anyone. Ten days thus passed by, days of storm and tempest, during which her son and his companions recrossed the Alps. They had left her on the 20th September, and it was not till she reached Paris on the 12th October that she became aware of the disastrous journey they had gone through, and how impossible it would have been for them to manage even as they did, had she been with them; indeed, she hardly could have lived through it. The description of this journey was written to Mrs. Shelley in a most graphic and picturesque letter by one of her son's companions. They were nearly drowned while crossing the lake in the diligence on a raft, during a violent storm. Next they were informed that the road of the Dazio Grande to Airolo was washed away sixty feet under the present torrent. They, with a guide, had to find their way over an unused mountain track, rendered most dangerous by the storm. They all lost shoes and stockings, and had to run on as best they could. Percy, with some others, had lost the track; but they, providentially, met the rest of the party at an inn at Piota, and from there managed to reach Airolo; and so they crossed the stupendous St. Gothard Pass, one of the wonders of the world.

Mrs. Shelley having at last recovered the letter from the Post Office, returned with her maid and a vetturino who had three Irish ladies with him, by way of Geneva, staying at Isola Bella. After passing the Lago Maggiore, a turn in the road shut the lake and Italy from her sight, and she proceeded on her journey with a heavy heart, as many a traveller has done and many more will do, the fascination of Italy under most circumstances being intense. Mary then describes one of the evils of Italy in its then divided state. The southern side of the Simplon belonged to the King of Sardinia, but its road led at once into Austrian boundary. The Sardinian sovereign, therefore, devoted this splendid pass to ruin to force people to go by Mont Cenis, and thus rendered the road most dangerous for those who were forced to traverse it. The journey over the Simplon proved most charming, and Mrs. Shelley was very much pleased with the civility of her vetturino, who managed everything admirably. Now, on her way to Geneva, she passed the same scenes she had lived first in with Shelley. She thus describes them:—

The far Alps were hid, the wide lake looked drear. At length I caught a glimpse of the scenes among which I had lived, when first I stepped out from childhood into life. There on the shores of Bellerive stood Diodati; and our humble dwelling, Maison Ohapuis, nestled close to the lake below. There were the terraces, the vineyards, the upward path threading them, the little port where our boat lay moored. I could mark and recognise a thousand peculiarities, familiar objects then, forgotten since—now replete with recollections and associations. Was I the same person who had lived there, the companion of the dead—for all were gone? Even my young child, whom I had looked upon as the joy of future years, had died in infancy. Not one hope, then in fair bud, had opened into maturity; storm and blight and death had passed over, and destroyed all. While yet very young, I had reached the position of an aged person, driven back on memory for companionship with the beloved, and now I looked on the inanimate objects that had surrounded me, which survived the same in aspect as then, to feel that all my life since is an unreal phantasmagoria—the shades that gathered round that scene were the realities, the substances and truth of the soul's life which I shall, I trust, hereafter rejoin.

Mary digresses at some length on the change of manners in the French since the revolution of 1830, saying that they had lost so much of their pleasant agreeable manner, their Monsieur and Madame, which sounded so pretty. From Geneva by Lyons, through Chalons, the diligence slowly carries her to Paris, and thence she shortly returned to England in October.

Mary's next tour with her son was in 1842, by way of Amsterdam, through Germany and Italy. From Frankfort she describes to a friend her journey with its various mishaps. After spending a charming week with friends in Hampshire, and then passing a day or two in London to bid farewell to old friends, Mrs. Shelley, her son, and Mr. Knox embarked for Antwerp on June 12, 1842. After the sea passage, which Mary dreaded, the pleasure of entering the quiet Scheldt is always great; but she does not seem to have recognised the charm of the Belgian or Dutch quiet scenery. With her love of mountains, these picturesque aspects seem lost on her; at least, she remarks that, "It is strange that a scene, in itself uninteresting, becomes agreeable to look at in a picture, from the truth with which it is depicted, and a perfection of colouring which at once contrasts and harmonizes the hues of sky and water." Mary does not seem to understand that the artist who does this selects the beauties of nature to represent. A truthful representation of a vulgarised piece of nature would be very painful for an artist to look on or to paint. The English or Italian villas of Lake Como, or the Riviera, would require a great deal of neglect by the artist not to vulgarize the glorious scenes round them; but this lesson has yet to be widely learnt in modern times, that beauty can never spoil nature, however humble; but no amount of wealth expended on a palace or mansion can make it fit for a picture, without the artist's feeling, any more than the beauties of Italy on canvas can be other than an eyesore without the same subtle power.

At Liège, fresh worries assailed the party. The difficulty of getting all their luggage, as well as a theft of sixteen pounds from her son's bedroom in the night, did not add to the pleasures of the commencement of their tour; but, as Mary said, the discomfort was nothing to what it would have been in 1840, when their means were far narrower, and she feels, "Welcome this evil so that it be the only one," for, as she says, one whose life had been so stained by tragedy could never regain a healthy tone, if that is needed not to fear for those we love. On reaching Cologne, the party went up the Rhine to Coblentz. As neither Mary nor her companions had previously done this, they were again much imposed upon by the steward. She recalls her former voyage with Shelley and Claire, when in an open boat they passed the night on the rapid river, "tethered" to a willow on the bank. When Frankfort is at length reached, they have to decide where to pass the summer. Kissingen is decided on, for Mrs. Shelley to try the baths. Here they take lodgings, and all the discomforts of trying to get the necessaries of life and some order, when quite ignorant of the language of the place, are amusingly described by Mrs. Shelley. The treatment and diet at the baths seem to have been very severe, nearly every usual necessary of life being forbidden by the Government in order to do justice to the efficacy of the baths.

Passing through various German towns their way to Leipsic, they stay at Weimar, where Mary rather startles the reader by remarking that she is not sure she would give the superiority to Goethe; that Schiller had always appeared to her the greater man, so complete. It is true she only knew the poets by translations, but the wonderful passages translated from Goethe by

Shelley might have impressed her more. Mary is much struck on seeing the tombs of the poets by their being placed in the same narrow chamber as the Princes, showing the genuine admiration of the latter for those who had cast a lustre on their kingdom, and their desire to share even in the grave the poet's renown. Mary, when in the country of Frederic the Great, shows little enthusiasm for that great monarch, so simple in his own life, so just, so beloved, and so surrounded by dangers which he overcame for the welfare of the country. What Frederic might have been in Napoleon's place after the Revolution it is difficult to conceive, or how he might have acted. Certainly not for mere self aggrandizement. But the tyrannies of the petty German Princes Mary justly does not pass over, such as the terrible story told in Schiller's *Cabal and Love*. She recalls how the Duke of Hesse-Cassel sold his peasants for the American war, to give with their pay jewels to his mistress, and how, on her astonishment being expressed, the servant replied they only cost seven thousand children of the soil just sent to America. On this Mary remarks:—"History fails fearfully in its duty when it makes over to the poet the record and memory of such an event; one, it is to be hoped, that can never be renewed. And yet what acts of cruelty and tyranny may not be reacted on the stage of the world which we boast of as civilised, if one man has uncontrolled power over the lives of many, the unwritten story of Russia may hereafter tell."

This seems to point to reminiscences of Claire's life in Russia. Mrs. Shelley also remarks great superiority in the comfort, order, and cleanliness in the Protestant over the Catholic parts of Germany, where liberty of conscience has been gained, and is profoundly touched on visiting Luther's chamber in the castle of Wartburg overlooking the Thuringian Forest.

Her visits to Berlin and Dresden, during the heat of summer, do not much strike the reader by her feeling for pictorial art. She is impressed by world-renowned pictures; but her remarks, though those of a clever woman, show that the love of nature, especially in its most majestic forms, does not give or imply love of art. The feeling for plastic art requires the emotion which runs through all art, and without which it is nothing, to be distinctly innate as in the artist, or to have been cultivated by surroundings and influence. True, it is apparently difficult always to trace the influence. There is no one step from the contemplation of the Alps to the knowledge of plastic art. Literary art does not necessarily understand pictorial art: it may profess to expound the latter, and the reader, equally or still more ignorant, fancies that he appreciates the pictorial art because he relishes its literary exposition. Surely a piece of true plastic art, constantly before a child for it to learn to love, would do more than much after study. The best of all ought to be given to children—music, poetry, art—for it is easier then to instil than later to eradicate. It is true these remarks may seem unnecessary with regard to Mary

Shelley, as, with all her real gifts and insight into poetry, she is most modest about her deficiencies in art knowledge, and is even apologetic concerning the remarks made in her letters, and for this her truth of nature is to be commended. In music, also, she seems more really moved by her own emotional nature than purely by the music; how, otherwise, should she have been disappointed at hearing *Masaniello*, while admiring German music, when Auber's grand opera has had the highest admiration from the chief German musicians? But she had not been previously moved towards it; that is the great difference between perception and acquired knowledge, and why so frequently the art of literature is mistaken for perception. But Mary used her powers justly, and drew the line where she was conscious of knowledge; she had real imagination of her own, and used the precious gift justifiably, and thus kept honour and independence, a difficult task for a woman in her position. She expresses pity for the travellers she meets, who simply are anxious to have "done" everything. She truly remarks:—"We must become a part of the scenes around us, and they must mingle and become a portion of us, or we see without seeing, and study without learning. There is no good, no knowledge, unless we can go out from and take some of the external into ourselves. This is the secret of mathematics as well as of poetry."

Their trip to Prague, and its picturesque position, afforded great pleasure to her. The stirring and romantic history is well described—history, as Shelley truly says, is a record of crime and misery. The first reformers sprang up in Bohemia. The martyrdom of John Huss did not extinguish his enlightening influence; and while all the rest of Europe was enslaved in darkness, Bohemia was free with a pure religion. But such a bright example might not last, and Bohemia became a province of the Empire, and not a hundred Protestants remain in the country now. The interesting story of St. John Nepomuk, the history of Wallenstein, with Schiller's finest tragedy, all lend their interest to Prague. In the journey through Bohemia and southern Germany, dirty and uncomfortable inns were conspicuous. The Lake of Gemünden much struck Mary with its poetic beauty, and she felt it was the place she should like to retreat to for a summer. From Ischl they went over the Brenner Pass of the Lago di Garda on to Italy. Mary was particularly struck by the beauties of Salzburg, with the immense plain half encircled by mountains crowned by castles, with the high Alps towering above all. She considered all this country superior to the Swiss Alps, and longed to pass months there some time. By this beautiful route they reached Verona, and then Venice. On the road to Venice Mary became aware (as we have already noted) of an intimate remembrance of each object, and each turn in the road. It was by this very road she entered Venice twenty-five years before with her dying child. She remarks that Shakspeare knew the feeling and endued the grief of Queen Constance with terrible reality; and, later, the poem of "The Wood Spurge" enforces the same sentiment. It was remarked by Holcroft that the notice the soul takes of objects presented to the eye in its hour of agony is a relief afforded by nature to permit the nerves to endure pain. On reaching Venice a search for lodgings was not successful; but two gentlemen, to whom they had introductions, found for the party an hotel within their still limited means; their bargain came to £9 a month each for everything included. They visited again the Rialto, and Mrs. Shelley observes:—"Often when here before, I visited this scene at this hour, or later, for often I expected Shelley's return from Palazzo Mocenigo till two or three in the morning. I watched the glancing of the oars, and heard the far song, and saw the palaces sleeping in the light of the moon, which veils by its deep shadows all that grieved the eye and hurt the heart in the decaying palaces of Venice; then I saw, as now I see, the bridge of the Rialto spanning the canal. All, all is the same; but, as the poet says,—'The difference to me.'"

She notices many of the most celebrated of the pictures in the Academia; and she had the good fortune of seeing St. Peter Martyr, which she misnames St. Peter the Hermit, out of its dark niche in the Church of Santi Giovanni e Paolo. She gives a very good description of Venetian life at the time, and much commends its family affection and family life as being of a much less selfish nature than in England; as she remarks truly, if a traveller gets into a vicious or unpleasant set in any country, it would not do to judge all the rest of the nation, by that standard—as she considered Shelley did when staying in Venice with Byron. The want of good education in Italy at that time she considers the cause of the ruling indolence, love-making with the young and money-keeping with the elder being the chief occupation. She gives a very good description of the noble families and their descent. Many of the Italian palaces preserved their pictures, and in the Palazzo Pisani Mary saw the Paul Veronese, now in the National Gallery, of "The family of Darius at the feet of Alexander." Mary's love of Venice grew, and she seems to have entertained serious ideas of taking a palace and settling there; but all the fancies of travellers are not realised. One moonlit evening she heard an old gondoliere challenge a younger one to alternate with him the stanzas of the *Gerusalemme*. The men stood on the Piazzetta beside the Laguna, surrounded by other gondolieri in the moonlight. They chanted "The death of Clorinda" and other favourite passages; and though, owing to Venetian dialect Mary could not follow every word, she was much impressed by the dignity and beauty of the scene. The Pigeons of St. Mark's existed then as now. Mary ended her stay in Venice by a visit to the Opera, and joined a party, by invitation, to accompany the Austrian Archduke to the Lido on his departure.

Mrs. Shelley much admired the expression in the early masters at Padua, though she does not mention Giotto. In Florence, the expense of the hotels again obliged her to go through the tiresome work of seeking apartments. They fortunately found sunny rooms, as the cold was intense. To cold followed rain, and she remarks:—"Walking is out of the question; and driving-how I at once envy and despise the happy rich who have carriages, and who use them only to drive every afternoon in the Cascine. If I could, I would visit every spot mentioned in Florentine history—visit its towns of old renown, and ramble amid scenes familiar to Dante, Boccaccio, Petrarch, and Machiavelli."

The descriptions of Ghirlandajo's pictures in Florence are very good. Mary now evidently studies art with great care and intelligence, and makes some very clever remarks appertaining to it. She is also able to call attention to the fact that Mr. Kirkup had recently made the discovery of the head of Dante Alighieri, painted by Giotto, on the wall of the Chapel of the Palace of the Podestà at Florence. The fact was mentioned by Vasari, and Kirkup was enabled to remove the whitewash and uncover this inestimable treasure. Giotto, in the act of painting this portrait, is the subject of one of the finest designs of the English school—alas! not painted in any form of fresco on an English wall.

From the art of Florence Mrs. Shelley turns to its history with her accustomed clear-headed method. Space will not admit all the interesting details, but her account of the factions and of the good work and terrible tragedies of the Carbonari is most interesting. The great equality in Florence is well noticed, accounting for the little real distress among the poor, and the simplicity of life of the nobles. She next enters into an account of modern Italian literature, which she ranks high, and hopes much from. The same struggle between romanticists and classicists existed as in other countries; and she classes Manzoni with Walter Scott, though admitting that he has not the same range of character. Mary and her party next proceeded by sea to Rome. Here, again, the glories of Italy and its art failed not to call forth eloquent remarks from Mary's pen; and her views, though at times somewhat contradictory, are always well expressed. She, at least, had a mind to appreciate the wonders of the Stanze, and to feel that genius and intellect are not out of their province in art. She only regrets that the great Italian art which can express so perfectly the religious sentiment and divine ecstasy did not attempt the grand feelings of humanity, the love which is faithful to death, the emotions such as Shakespeare describes. While this wish exists, and there are artists who can carry it out, art is not dead. After a very instructive chapter on the modern history of the Papal States, we again find Mary among the scenes dearest to her heart and her nature: her next letter is dated from Sorrento. She feels herself to be in Paradise; and who that has been in that wonderful country would not sympathise with her enthusiasm! To be carried up the heights to Ravello, and to see the glorious panorama around, she considered, surpassed all her previous most noble experiences. Ravello, with its magnificent cathedral covered with mosaics, is indeed a sight to have seen; the road to

Amalfi, the ruinous paper mills in the ravine, the glorious picturesqueness, are all "well expressed and understood." Mrs. Shelley seems to have considered June (1844) the perfection of weather for Naples.

CHAPTER XVII.

LAST YEARS.

This last literary work by Mrs. Shelley, of which she herself speaks slightingly as a poor performance, was noticed about the time of its publication as an interesting and truthful piece of writing by an authority on the subject. Mrs. Shelley's very modest and retiring disposition gave her little confidence in herself, and she seems to have met, with various discouraging remarks from acquaintances; she used to wonder afterwards that she was not able to defend herself and suppress impertinence. This last book is spoken of by Mary as written to help an unfortunate person whose acquaintance Claire had made in Paris while staying in some capacity in that city with Lady Sussex Lennox. A title has a factitious prestige with some people, and certainly in this case the acquaintance which at first seemed advantageous to Mary proved to be much the contrary, both in respect of money and of peace of mind; but, before referring further to this subject, we must explain that the year 1844 brought with it a perhaps questionable advantage for her.

Sir Timothy Shelley, who had been ailing for some while, and whom Percy Shelley had visited from time to time at Field Place, having become rather a favourite with the old gentleman, now reached the bourne of life—he was ninety. His death in April 1844 brought his grandson Percy Florence to the baronetcy. That portion of the estate which had been entailed previous to Sir Bysshe's proposed rearrangement of the entire property now came to Mrs. Shelley by her husband's will. Owing to the poet's having refused to join in the entail, the larger portion of the property would not under any circumstances, as we have before mentioned, have devolved on him.

A sum of £80,000 is mentioned by the different biographers of Shelley as the probable value of the minor estate entailed on him, of which he had the absolute right of disposal. This estate, on Sir Timothy's death, was found to be burdened to the extent of £50,000, which Mary borrowed on mortgage at 3-1/2 per cent. This large sum included £13,000 due to Lady Shelley for "the pittance" Mary had received; £4,500 to John Shelley for a mortgage Shelley signed to pay his debts, probably for the £2,000 borrowed on leaving Marlow, when he paid all his debts there; so that if any trifle was left unpaid on that occasion, it must have been from oversight and want of dunning, as he undoubtedly left there with sufficient money, having also resold his house for £1,000. A jointure had to be paid Lady Shelley of £500 a year. The different legacies still due in 1844 were £6,000 to Ianthe, two sums of £6,000 each to Claire, £2,000 to Hogg, £2,500 to Peacock. These various sums mounting up to £40,000, the remaining £10,000 can easily have been swallowed up by other post-obits and legal expenses. Two sums of £6,000 each left to his two sons who died, and £2,000 left to Lord Byron, had lapsed to the estate. Mrs. Shelley's first care was to raise the necessary money and pay all the outstanding obligations. Her chief anxiety through her struggles had always been not to incur debts; her next thought was to give an annual pension of £50 to her brother's widow, and £200 a year (afterwards reduced to £120) to Leigh Hunt. This was her manner of deriving immediate pleasure from her inheritance. By her husband's will, executed in 1817, everything, "whether in possession, reversion, remainder, or expectancy," was left to her; but as she always mentioned her son, Sir Percy, as acting with herself, and said that owing to the embarrassed condition of the estate they intended to share all in common for a time, it is evident that Mary had made her son's interest her first duty.

The estate had brought £5,000 the previous year, and this would agree, deducting £1,750 for interest on mortgage, and £500 Lady Shelley's jointure, in reducing their income to a little below £3,000 a year, as Mrs. Shelley stated. Field Place was let in the first instance for sixty pounds a year, it was so damp. Mrs. Shelley continued with, her son to live at Putney till 1846. They had tried Putney in 1839, and towards the end of 1843 she took a house there, the White Cottage, Lower Richmond Road, Putney. Mary thus describes it:— "Our cot is on the banks of the Thames, not looking on it, but the garden-gate opens on the towing-path. It has a nice little garden, but sadly out of order. It is shabbily furnished, and has no spare room, except by great contrivance, if at all; so, perforce, economy will be the order of the day. It is secluded but cheerful, at the extreme verge of Putney, close to Barnes Common; just the situation Percy desired. He has bought a boat."

Mrs. Shelley moved into this house shortly after the visit to Claire in Paris, referred to at the commencement of this chapter.

Her life in London, in spite of a few very good friends, often appeared solitary to her; for, as she herself observes, those who produce and give original work to the world require the social contact of their fellow-beings. Thus, saddened by the neglect which she experienced, she tried to counteract it by sympathising with those less fortunate than herself; but this, also, is at times a very difficult task to carry out single-handed beyond a certain point.

During this visit to Paris in 1843 she had the misfortune to meet, at the house of Lady Sussex Lennox, an Italian adventurer of the name of Gatteschi. They had known some people of that name formerly in Florence, as noted in Claire's diary of 1820; and this may have caused them to take a more special interest in him. Suffice it to say, that he appeared to be in the greatest distress, and at the same time was considered by Mary and Claire to have the *éclat* of "good birth," and also to have talents, which, if they got but a fair chance, might raise him to any post of eminence. These ideas continued for some time; on one occasion he helped Mrs. Shelley with her literary work, finding the historical passages for *Rambles in Germany and Italy*. She and Claire used to contrive to give him small sums of money, in some delicate way, so as not to wound his feelings, as he would die of mortification. He was invited over to England in 1844, under the idea that he might obtain some place as tutor in a family, and he brought over MSS. of his own, which were thought highly of. While in England Gatteschi lodged with Mr. Knox, who had travelled with Mrs. Shelley and her son, as a friend of the latter. Mr. Knox seems to have been at that time on friendly terms with Gatteschi, though Mrs. Shelley regretted that her son did not take to him. With all the impulse of a generous nature, she spared no pains to be of assistance to the Italian, and evidently must have written imprudently gushing letters at times to this object of her commiseration. Whilst Mary was poor Gatteschi must have approached sentimental gratitude; she says later, "He cannot now be wishing to marry me, or he would not insult me." In fact he had proposed to marry her when she came into her money. Gatteschi waited his time, he aimed at larger sums of money. Failing to get these by fair means, the scoundrel began to use threats of publishing her correspondence with him. In 1845 he was said to be "ravenous for money," and, knowing how Mary had yielded to vehement letters on former occasions, and had at first answered him imprudently, instead of at once putting his letters into legal hands, the villain made each fresh letter a tool to serve his purpose. He thus worked upon her sensitive nature and dread of ridicule, especially at a time when she more than ever wished to stand well with the world and the society which she felt it her son's right to belong to—her son, who had never failed in his duty, and who, she said, was utterly without vice, although at times she wished he had more love of reading and steady application.

It is easy to see now how perfectly innocent, although Quixotically generous, Mary Shelley was; but it can also be discerned how difficult it would have been to stop the flood of social mirth and calumny, had more of this subject been, made public. Mary, knowing this only too well, bitterly deplored it, and accused herself of folly in a way that might even now deceive a passing thinker; but it has been the pleasant task of the writer to make this subject perfectly clear to herself, and some others.

It must be added that the letters in question, written by Mrs. Shelley to Gatteschi, were obtained by a requisition of the French police under the pretext of political motives: Gatteschi had been known to be mixed up with an insurrection in Bologna. Mr. Knox, who managed this affair for Mrs. Shelley, showed the talents of an incipient police magistrate.

The whole of Mary's correspondence with Claire Clairmont is very cordial. Mary did her best to help her from time to time in her usual generous manner, and evidently gave her the best advice in her power. We find her regretting at times Claire's ill-health, sending her carriage to her while in Osnaburgh Street, and so on. She strongly urged her to come to England to settle about the investment of her money, telling her that one £6,000 she cannot interfere with, as Shelley had left it for an annuity which could not be lost or disposed of; but that the other £6,000 she can invest where she likes. At one time Mary tells her of a good investment she has heard of in an opera-box, but that she must act for herself, as it is too dangerous a matter to give advice in.

In 1845 Mary Shelley visited Brighton for her health, her nerves having been much shaken by the anxiety she had gone through. While there she mentioned seeing Mr. and Mrs. John Shelley at the Theatre, but they took no notice of her. When Mrs. Shelley went over Field Place after Sir Timothy's death, Lady Shelley had expressed herself to a friend as being much pleased with her, and said she wished she had known her before: Mary on hearing this exclaimed, "Then why on earth didn't she?" In 1846 they moved from Putney to Chester Square, and in the summer Mary went to Baden for her health. From here again she wrote how glad she was to be away from the mortifications of London, and that she detested Chester Square. Her health from this time needed frequent change. In 1847, she moved to Field Place; she found it damp, but visits to Brighton and elsewhere helped to keep up her gradually failing health. The next year she had the satisfaction of seeing her son married to a lady (Mrs. St. John) in every way to her liking. A letter received by Mrs. Shelley from her daughter-in-law while on her wedding tour, and enclosed to Claire, shows how she wished the latter to partake in the joy she felt at the happy marriage of her son. Mary now had not only a son to love, but a daughter to care for her, and the pleasant duty was not unwillingly performed, for the lady speaks of her to this day with emotion.

From this time there is little to record. We find Mary in 1849 inviting Willie Clairmont, Claire's nephew, to see her at Field Place, where she was living with her son and his wife. In the same year they rather dissuaded Claire, who was then at Maidstone, from a somewhat wild project which she entertained, that of going to California. The ground of dissuasion was still wilder than the project, for it was just now said the hoped-for gold had turned out to be merely sulphate of iron. The house in Chester Square had been given up in 1848, and another was taken at 77, Warwick Square, before the marriage of Sir Percy, and thence at the end of that year Mary writes of an improvement in her health, but there was still a tendency to neuralgic rheumatism. The life-long nerve strain for a time was relaxed, but without doubt the tension had been too strong, and loving care could not prevail beyond a certain point. The next year the son and his wife took the drooping Mary to Nice for her health, and a short respite was given; but the pressure could not much longer remain. The strong brain, and tender, if once too impassioned heart, failed on February 21, 1851, and nothing remained but a cherished memory of the devoted daughter and mother, and the faithful wife of Shelley.